the

noodle

cook

book

the noodle cook book

Delicious recipes for crispy, stir-fried, boiled, sweet, spicy, hot, and cold noodles

Kurumi Hayter

APPLE

A   QUINTET   BOOK

Published by The Apple Press
6 Blundell Street
London N7 9BH

ISBN 1-85076-670-3

This book was designed and produced by
Quintet Publishing Limited
6 Blundell Street
London N7 9BH

Creative Director: **RICHARD DEWING**
Designer: **SIMON BALLEY**
Senior Editor: **LAURA SANDELSON**
Editor: **CAROLINE BALL**
Photographer: **DAVID ARMSTRONG**

Typeset in Great Britain by
Central Southern Typesetters, Eastbourne
Manufactured in Singapore by
Bright Arts (Pte) Ltd
Printed in Singapore by
Star Standard Industries (Pte) Ltd

DEDICATION
For my husband, Simon

contents

introduction

Above
*Bunching
noodles,
Thailand*

Y ou will find them served from a stall by the roadside in the wastes of northern China, in crowded ramen shops in the heart of Tokyo's financial district, on the beach in the sandy resorts of Thailand and in villages on the sub-tropical islands of Indonesia. In south and east Asia, the noodle is ubiquitous. In most Asian nations, it challenges rice as the main staple. Prepared in as little as five minutes, the humble noodle could even stake a claim to the title of the world's first and fastest fast food, though real noodle dishes bear no resemblance to the bland, anaemic-looking strands lurking in pot noodle tubs on supermarket shelves. Noodles are never pre-cooked, only prepared while you wait and served fresh and steaming hot. Noodles are nothing if not versatile. They can be made into a nourishing and filling meal accompanied by a broth to warm the coldest night, or made into a nest filled with stir-fried meat or vegetables for a hearty meal. They can be served as a salad, or over ice in a thin soy-based sauce as a refreshing summer treat. Noodles come in a wide range of types, thicknesses and textures, from the delicate filaments of Thai vermicelli to finger-thick Japanese udon.

Noodles are high in carbohydrates, low in fat and quickly prepared. With a high proportion of noodles and vegetables to animal products, they are a very healthy dietary alternative. With so much going for them, it is not surprising that noodles are beginning to catch on in a big way in the West. I hope reading this book will show you why.

Right
*Noodles
drying,
China*

types of noodles

There are close to twenty different varieties of noodles available, made from basic ingredients such as wheat, buckwheat and rice flour. The different varieties require different treatment. Some noodles are best fried while others make a better contribution to a meal when boiled and served in a broth. Some can be made at home.

Soaking and cooking times given here are approximate, and may vary from brand to brand – check the instructions on the packet.

egg noodles

Egg noodles are made from wheat flour, egg and water, and are eaten widely over south-west Asia both in soups and as stir-fried dishes. They commonly come in thin or medium thicknesses, and can be bought fresh or dried. Fresh egg noodles or fresh Japanese *ramen* noodles are best especially for hot noodle soups on account of their texture. Egg noodles can also be deep fried to make crispy noodles. Japanese steamed noodles are especially suitable for stir-fried dishes. Fresh egg noodles are sold in Chinese stores and fresh Japanese *ramen* noodles and steamed noodles are available from shops stocking Japanese foods. Other dried egg noodles are easily obtained from supermarkets.

Fresh and steamed egg noodles should be eaten within two or three days and kept in the fridge or frozen. Dried egg noodles can be kept over a long period as long as they are in an airtight pack or container. Japanese fresh *ramen* or steamed noodles are often sold in a packet with a ready-made soup or sauce.

cooking times

thin (fresh or dried) egg noodles

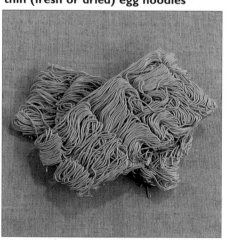

boil for 3 minutes

medium (fresh or dried) egg noodles

boil for 4 minutes

Japanese fresh *ramen*

boil for 2–3 minutes

Japanese steamed egg noodles

rinse in boiling water

udon, soba and somen

Udon is mainly eaten in Japan and Korea and made from wheat flour and water. *Udon* noodles come in various thicknesses, both round and flat. *Udon* is sold at Chinese and Japanese supermarkets in fresh, parboiled or dried forms. You can even make fresh *udon* at home (see page 24), but it requires professional skill to get exactly the right texture. It is suitable for hot noodle soups, cold dishes and stir-fries.

Soba possesses its own distinctive flavour. It is made from buckwheat and plain flour, and is very nutritious, rich in protein and lecithin. *Soba* is sold fresh, parboiled or dried at Japanese and Chinese stores, but hot dried *soba* is the most easy to find. It is served in hot noodle soups or as a cold dish.

Somen is made from wheat flour and water and is only sold dried. Care should be taken handling *somen* as it is very fragile. *Somen* is commonly used for cold summer dishes, but can also be used in hot noodle soups.

cooking times

freshly made *udon*

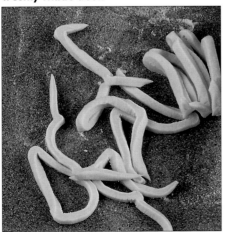

boil for 13–15 minutes

parboiled fresh *udon*

boil for 3 minutes

flat *udon* (*kishimen*)

boil for 3–4 minutes

dried *udon*

boil for 7–15 minutes (depending on thickness)

dried *soba*

boil for 5–6 minutes

somen

boil for 1–2 minutes

rice noodles

Rice vermicelli is made from rice flour and water and is very fragile. It is sold in dried form at most supermarkets and Chinese stores. Rice vermicelli is deep fried to make crispy noodles and is also used in soups and stir-fries.

Rice stick noodles (or *ho fun* in Chinese, *sen men* in Thai) vary in the thickness and shape. They are made from rice flour, starch and water. Fresh steamed flat rice noodles are sold at Chinese supermarkets and should be used within a couple of days of the purchase and stored in the fridge.

soaking times

rice vermicelli

3–5 minutes in warm water

rice stick noodles

2–5 minutes in warm water

fresh steamed flat rice noodles

rinse with hot water

bean thread noodles

Bean thread vermicelli or noodles, also known as transparent, cellophane or mung bean thread noodles, are made from mung bean flour. They are sold at Chinese stores in dried form and look similar to rice vermicelli. However, these noodles are tougher than rice vermicelli and are used for soups. hot pots, braised dishes and in stir-fries.

soaking time

bean thread vermicelli

5 minutes in boiling water

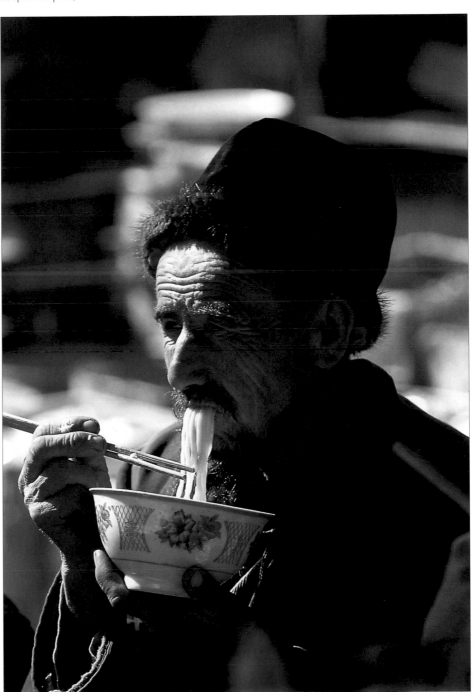

Right

Eating ("slurping") noodles, Xinjiang, China

how to prepare and cook noodles

Cooking noodles is simplicity itself. All that is needed is a large pan of water. The essential thing about noodles, like spaghetti, is to get the texture right, which means care should be taken to avoid overcooking. Timing is another important consideration. The other elements of the dish should all be ready so that once the noodles are cooked everything can be served without delay, as cooked noodles tend to stick together if left for any time after cooking.

boiling method

ramen and egg noodles

Bring plenty of water to the boil in a pan, then add the noodles. Stir a couple of times to prevent the noodles sticking together.

udon and soba

Bring plenty of water to the boil in a pan. Add the *udon* or *soba* and stir a couple of times. When the water is about to boil, add a small cup of water to bring the temperature down. When the water comes back to the boil, add more water. Rinse well under cold water and drain.

somen

As with egg noodles and *udon*, the only thing you need is boiling water. Immerse the *somen* and stir a couple of times. When the water is coming to the boil, add a small cup of water only once. As the water is about to boil over, it is ready. Rinse well under cold water.

soaking method

Rice noodles need to be soaked in warm water and bean thread noodles are soaked in boiling water. Both types of noodles are then rinsed with cold water and drained. The soaking time varies according to the kinds and thickness of the noodles (refer to the instruction on the packet).

Above Left

Boiling egg
noodles

Above
Right
Deep-frying
rice
vermicelli

deep-frying (to make crispy noodles)

egg noodles

First boil in hot water (see above), then rinse and drain. The noodles should then be separated, spread out on a tray and dried well. Heat the oil to 180°C/350°F and fry small amounts at a time, using chopsticks or tongs to turn them. Deep fry until golden brown. When cooked, they should be drained on kitchen paper.

rice vermicelli

Rice vermicelli can be deep fried without any preparation. Fry only small amounts at a time. After only a few seconds the vermicelli becomes puffy and white; take it out and drain on kitchen paper.

serving and eating noodles

Noodles absorb liquid very rapidly, which is why it is essential not to overcook them. By the same token, it is important that hot noodle soup dishes are served and eaten as soon as they are ready. So only pour the broth over noodles just before you are going to eat them. Don't worry about making a slurping sound when eating noodles, that is not only unavoidable but part of the fun!

note

All recipes are for four servings unless indicated otherwise.
Metric and imperial conversions are approximate.
Spoon measures are level.

utensils

The utensils for cooking noodles are basic and all derived from the Chinese kitchen. One of the most useful and simple pieces of equipment to have on hand is a wok. This versatile pan can be used for stir-frying, deep-frying, braising, boiling and steaming. The wok is traditionally made from iron, though modern non-stick versions are also available. If you do not possess a wok, a large, deep frying pan can be used as a substitute.

how to care for a wok

After use, the wok should be scrubbed well with a brush in hot water. Do not use washing-up liquid as the wok's surface should remain oily to prevent rusting. After hand drying, return the wok to the hob for about a minute, to dry the surface thoroughly. When dry, dip a piece of kitchen paper in a little oil and wipe the inside of the wok as a further preventative against rusting. Only when a wok has become rusty should you use washing-up liquid.

using a wok

The wok should be heated before oil is added. To be hot enough for stir-frying the oil should be heated until it begins to smoke, which prevents the ingredients from sticking to the wok.

Below *Two designs of wok, one with the traditional long wooden handle and the other with two carrying handles. The brush may be used to oil woks, and the strainers are useful accessories for some recipes*

techniques and preparation

"Chopstick cultures" demand that most food be chopped or sliced into bite-sized pieces before cooking. Usually, all ingredients, whether they be meat, fish or vegetable, are cut into the same size. As the origins of the noodle stem from Chinese cuisine, most noodle-based dishes follow this basic precept even though the fork and spoon are used in place of chopsticks in countries such as Thailand and Indonesia.

Left Most noodle dishes require ingredients to be chopped or sliced in order to facilitate easy eating with chopsticks

cutting techniques

mincing

First, the meat or vegetable is thinly sliced and then chopped very finely into mince.

dicing

Vegetables and tofu are cut thickly, then cut again into small cubes.

random cutting

Vegetables are cut and rolled at the same time in order to produce the random effect.

matchsticks

Vegetables are cut into matchstick-sized pieces.

shredding

Vegetables are thinly sliced first, then shredded more finely than matchsticks.

diagonal slicing

Vegetables are sliced thinly on a slant. This technique is often used before shredding.

slanted cutting

It is not easy to cut meat into fine slices by yourself. If your butcher will not do this for you the easiest method is as follows. Half freeze the meat, then cut, slanting the knife in the direction of the cut to get the thinnest slices.

glossary

Bamboo shoots When bamboo has just appeared above the ground, it is edible and collected in large quantities. Fresh bamboo shoots are widely used in oriental countries. Parboiled and canned bamboo shoots are widely available. Sliced tinned bamboo shoots are used in this book. Cooked dried bamboo shoots (*shinachiku*) originated in China but are now frequently used as a garnish for *ramen* dishes in Japan. *Shinachiku* is available from Japanese stores.

Bean curd (*tofu*) Bean curd is made from soya beans and has a soft texture. It is a very healthy food, high in protein and low in fat. There are two types available, firm cotton tofu and fragile silken tofu. Cotton tofu is used in this book and widely available from large supermarkets, healthfood shops and oriental food shops. If you cannot use it all, immerse the tofu in water in a container and keep in the fridge where it will last for a few days. The water must be changed daily.

Bean curd sheet (*abura-age*) Abura-age is a sheet of deep-fried bean curd, also made from soya beans. It is used in Japanese cooking and can be obtained from Japanese grocers. Do not confuse it with Chinese dried bean curd. Before use, always rinse it with hot water to wash off any excess oil. *Abura-age* can be frozen.

Black bean sauce Black beans are salted and fermented with spices to produce this sauce. It has a strong salty taste and is used widely in south-east Asian and Chinese cooking. Black bean sauce is available at supermarkets and oriental grocers; the taste can vary depending on the brand.

Bonito flakes (*katuso-bushi*) Bonito is a member of the tuna family. When dried and grated into flakes, it is one of the essential ingredients in Japanese cuisine. It is mainly used for making Japanese stock, but also as an ingredient in other dishes and as a garnish. Available from Japanese grocers, large supermarkets and healthfood shops. Keep it stored in an airtight tin.

Bowles' mint (*oba*) The leaves of the *oba* plant are large, round and mid green, and taste of spearmint. Fresh *oba* leaves are used extensively for mixing with other ingredients or as a garnish. They are available at Japanese grocers.

Candle nut Round candle nuts are the fruit of the candleberry tree. They are used crushed or ground as thickening agents with other ingredients. Macadamia nuts can be used as a fine substitute.

Cha siu sauce This is the marinade sauce used for making Chinese barbecued pork. It is a blend of many ingredients, including Chinese five spices, honey, sugar, soy sauce, rice wine and garlic. *Cha siu* sauce is sold at oriental stores.

Chilli bean sauce (*toban djan*) *Toban djan* is a thick, dark reddish sauce, made from chilli, soya beans and soy sauce. It is used for spicing up Chinese dishes. Chilli bean sauce is available from large supermarkets or oriental food stores.

Chilli oil Chilli oil is a red-coloured oil, made from ground chillies. It is used for cooking, as a spice, and can be added to some dips. Chilli oil is available from supermarkets as well as from oriental grocers.

Chilli sauce (*sambal oelek*) *Sambal oelek* is an Indonesian chilli paste, made from crushed red chillies. It is used for cooking as well as a condiment. *Sambal oelek* is sold at Asian grocers.

Chinese green chives These are leafy stems about 30 cm/12 in long. As a substitute, the green part of spring onions can be used. Chinese green chives are sold at Chinese grocers.

Chilli oil

Oba

lemon grass

Chinese rice wine There are several kinds of rice wine, the most famous of which is Shaoxing, used for drinking and cooking. In this book, clear rice wine is used.

Coconut milk Coconut milk is a thick cream made from coconut flesh, not the watery fluid from the middle of a fresh coconut. It is available in tins or as a powder, and the quality does vary. It is sold at large supermarkets, Asian shops and Indian grocers.

Crispy onion/fried onion Thinly sliced onion shallow fried until brown and crisp is not easy to make at home, but is sold in supermarkets and oriental grocers. It is used as a garnish.

Daikon or mooli *Daikon* is a long, white radish, also known as mooli in the west. It is eaten raw, just grated, or cooked. Mooli is a slightly narrower radish and, being grown in Europe, is easier to obtain.

Dried black ear fungus A mushroom used in Chinese dishes, black ear fungus is usually sold dried and have to be soaked in warm water before use; it expands to about four times its dried size. It has a firm texture. Dried black ear fungus is sold at oriental grocers.

Dried kelp (konbu) *Konbu*, dark strips of kelp, is one of the most essential ingredients for making Japanese stock. It is usually dried and dark green in colour. It should be wiped with a damp cloth before use. *Konbu* is available from large supermarkets, healthfood stores and Japanese stores.

Dried shrimps Do not confuse these with dried shrimp paste; dried shrimps are salty, hard, whole shrimps, used for adding extra flavour. Sometimes they are soaked in water before use. Dried shrimps are very different from the Japanese variety. You can find them in Chinese and Thai food stores.

Dried shrimp paste (belacan) *Belacan* is a fermented shrimp paste with a very characteristic, strong smell. Before use, *belacan* has to be fried. It is sold at Chinese and Thai grocers.

Enoki mushrooms *Enoki* mushrooms are slender, creamy in colour with tiny caps. They grow from a dense set of roots which must be cut off prior to use. *Enoki* mushrooms are available from Japanese and Chinese stores.

Fish balls Fish balls are made from pounded fish paste and are slightly smaller than golf balls in size.

Fish sauce (nam pla) *Nam pla* is a light brown liquid made from salted, fermented fish. It is one of the essential seasonings in Thai cuisine and, as you would imagine, has a seaside, fishy smell. *Nam pla* is sold at oriental grocers.

Galangal *Galangal* is a cousin of ginger; it is slightly harder and the aroma is a little different. Fresh ginger may be substituted but use half the amount.

Gobo Gobo is a narrow, long, edible root akin to the burdock. When using fresh, scrape with a knife and soak in vinegared water to prevent discoloration. It is full of fibre and used in Japanese cooking; it is available from Japanese grocers.

Japanese fermented soya beans (natto) *Natto* is the end product of fermenting soya beans. It is very sticky and has a smell which some find offputting. It is not every Japanese's favourite, but is very good for you, being high in fibre and protein.

Japanese fish cake (kamaboko) *Kamaboko* is a Japanese version of a fish cake. It is made from pulped white fish gelled into a firm semi-cylindrical shape. It is mainly eaten sliced, accompanied by some soy sauce.

miso

dried shrimps

Japanese fermented soy beans (natto)

Japanese rice wine (sake) The taste of Japanese rice wine is very different from its Chinese equivalent. *Sake* is made from fermented steamed rice, water and enzyme, and tastes sweeter. It is used for both cooking and drinking. *Sake* is sold in large supermarkets, some off-licences and oriental stores.

Kaffir lime leaves Kaffir lime leaves are widely used as a flavouring in Thai cuisine, and also used in some Malaysian and Indonesian dishes. They are sold fresh or dried at Asian grocers and large supermarkets.

Lemon grass Lemon grass is used in Thai, Malay and Indonesian cooking to add the flavour of citrus to dishes. it is sold at supermarkets and Asian grocers.

Mirin Made from rice, water and alcohol (but with a low alcohol content), Mirin is used to enhance sweetness in Japanese cooking. It is sold at Japanese and Chinese grocers.

Miso paste *Miso* paste is another soya product, made from fermented cooked soya beans. It is quite salty and used a lot in Japanese cuisine. There are two types of *miso*, white and red. In this book, red *miso* is used as it has a stronger flavour than the mild, white version. *Miso* is sold in large supermarkets, healthfood stores and oriental grocers. It should be stored in the fridge where it will last for several months.

Mustard greens Mustard greens are used for Chinese dishes. Fresh mustard greens are available from Chinese grocers, or spinach can be used as a substitute.

Myoga *Myoga* is a relation of the ginger plant. It is the *myoga* buds that are eaten, either raw, pickled or as a garnish in Japanese dishes.

Nameko mushrooms *Nameko* mushrooms are small with light brown caps and have a slippery outer coating.

Nori *Nori* is blackish green laver seaweed dried into paper-thin sheets. Some *nori* has to be grilled over a gas ring for a few seconds, until the colour of the *nori* changes to green. *Nori* should be kept in an airtight container and handled with care as it flakes easily. It is sold at large supermarkets, healthfood shops and oriental food shops.

Oyster sauce Oyster sauce is made from extract of oysters, salt and soy sauce. Oyster sauce has a characteristic smell and is often used for flavouring dishes in Chinese cuisine. It is sold in supermarkets and oriental grocers.

Palm sugar Made from the sap of the coconut palm, palm sugar is used throughout south-east Asia. It is light brown in colour and has got a distinguishing sweet toffee smell. Palm sugar is available from Asian shops, or brown sugar can be used as a substitute.

Red pickled ginger (beni-shouga) Slivered ginger is pickled with a little sugar and vinegar and used as a garnish in Japanese dishes. It is sold at Japanese grocers.

Satoimo *Satoimo* is a potato with dark brown, hairy skin. The flesh is white and slippery. To prepare, wash with a brush under the tap and peel – wear gloves as the flesh can cause an itching sensation. *Satoimo* is a common ingredient in Japanese cookery. It is sold in large supermarkets and oriental grocers.

Sesame oil Sesame oil is made from sesame seeds and has a distinctive aroma. It is used as a flavouring and is easily available.

Sesame paste/sauce Made from pounded sesame seeds and a creamy light brown in colour, sesame paste has an aromatic smell. Peanut butter can be used as a substitute but sesame paste is available from large supermarkets or oriental grocers.

Seven flavours chilli powder (shichimi) *Shichimi* is a Japanese chilli powder, ground and blended with a mixture of red chilli pepper, black pepper, sesame seeds, poppy seeds, nori, hemp seeds and *sansho* pepper. It is used as a seasoning over *udon* or *soba* noodle soup and other Japanese dishes. *Shichimi* is sold at Japanese and Chinese grocers.

Shiitake mushrooms *Shiitake* mushrooms are widely used in oriental cooking. They have a characteristic smoky smell, especially after soaking. Soak dried mushrooms in warm water for about 20 minutes and remove the stems. Fresh mushrooms are available in season from supermarkets, healthfood shops and oriental food stores.

Chinese mushrooms (nameko)

nori

seven flavours chilli powder

Shimeji mushrooms *Shimeji* mushrooms grow in short, stumpy clusters from a simple root. The stalks are creamy at the base gradually becoming greyish brown toward the cap. They have a mild, subtle flavour. They form a frequent ingredient in Japanese cooking. Cut off the root before use. They can be obtained from Japanese stores.

Soured plums (*umeboshi*) *Umeboshi* are green plums which have been salted with red shiso leaves and are a traditional Japanese preserved food. They taste quite sour, so a little goes a long way. Some Japanese still make *umeboshi* at home. They are sold in cartons in Japanese grocers.

Soy sauce Many countries in Asia produce their own soy sauce, made from soya beans, salt, wheat flour and water first fermented and then brewed. Three kinds of soy sauce are used in this book:
Japanese soy sauce: similar to light soy sauce, though less salty.
Light soy sauce: a Chinese product, quite salty and used frequently for flavouring.
Dark soy sauce: much darker than the other two as it is aged longer. It is less salty and has a hint of sweetness.
   All these soy sauces are widely available.

Straw mushrooms Straw mushrooms are oval shape with dark brown caps and used in China and other oriental countries. They are sold tinned in large supermarkets and oriental grocers.

wasabi

Tamarind Dried tamarind pulp is first soaked in water, then strained to squeeze out the dark juice. It is used to sour south-east Asian food as well as Indian dishes. Tamarind pulp is sold at Indian and Asian grocers.

Thai red curry paste Red curry paste is made from the combination of red chillies, lemon grass, shallots, garlic, shrimp paste, galangal, coriander, fennel and other spices. It has a hot but sour taste quite distinct from Indian curry. Thai curry paste is sold in large supermarkets and Asian food shops.

Wakame seaweed *Wakame* is a green seaweed, thinner than kelp (*konbu*), and is used in Japanese cooking. Dried *wakame* has to be soaked in water for 5 minutes or in hot water for 2 minutes before use. It is easier to store and more readily available, from large supermarkets, healthfood shops and Japanese grocers, than fresh salted *wakame*.

Wasabi *Wasabi* is a Japanese horseradish which grows only in clean water; it is the pungent root that is edible. Fresh *wasabi* is grated and used as a garnish, but even in Japan it is expensive and difficult to purchase. *Wasabi* powder or paste is commonly used and available from Japanese and Chinese grocers.

wakame seaweed

Water chestnuts The water chestnut is actually a bulb, very similar in shape to a chestnut but unrelated. Water chestnuts have a crunchy texture and are used in Chinese dishes. Peeled, white water chestnuts are easily available tinned in large supermarkets and oriental grocers.

Wonton wrappers Wonton wrappers are paper-thin, small square sheets made from flour, egg and water. They are used for wrapping a filling of minced meat, vegetables or prawns, then fried, steamed or boiled in soup. Wontons originated in China, but are also widely eaten in other Asian countries. Fresh or frozen wonton wrappers are available from Chinese grocers.

Yakisoba sauce *Yakisoba* sauce is a dark brown sauce, used in Japanese stir-fried noodles. Japanese brown sauce is a good substitute or blend your own *yakisoba* sauce from the recipe on page 88. As a last resort, ordinary brown sauce could be used. *Yakisoba* sauce and Japanese brown sauce are sold at Japanese grocers.

Yam (*yama-imo*) The yam is a relation of the sweet potato. It varies in shape and size and is white in colour. When peeled, the yam begins to ooze and become sticky, so when you grate it, expose only a small amount of the flesh at a time.

Yellow bean sauce Made from fermented yellow beans with flour and salt, yellow bean sauce is used in Chinese cookery. It is thick and salty but with a hint of sweetness. Yellow bean sauce is sold in jars in supermarkets and oriental grocers.

hot noodle soups

Hot noodle soups make for warm bodies on cold windy days. Ramen *is the Japanese name for Chinese noodles. Thai, Malaysian and Indonesian noodle soups are quite different from Chinese and Japanese hot noodle soups – a spicy, sour taste dominates their broth and chilli is one of the most important ingredients.* Udon *and* soba *are mainly eaten in Japan. Once you have a good stock for these hot noodle recipes, you are half way towards producing a delicious, wholesome dish.*

making fresh udon

Making udon noodles is usually a professional job in Japan, and both fresh and dried udon are widely available in the shops. A key point to successful home-made udon is good, hard kneading. If you cannot bring yourself to use your feet and tread on the dough, you can knead by hand. Just make sure you knead well. When you knead the dough with your feet, remember to take off your shoes! The texture of freshly made udon is firm and quite different from dried udon. Boiling time for freshly made udon is 14–15 minutes. They can be refrigerated in a plastic bag for up to three days.

1. Adding water to flour

2. Kneading *udon* into a round

3. Slicing *udon* into strips

2 tbsp salt
200 ml/7 fl oz water
150 g/6 oz strong flour
250 g/9 oz plain flour
plain flour for dusting

● Dissolve the salt in the water in a cup. Sift the strong and plain flours together into a large bowl. Add the salted water little by little, mixing with chopsticks or a fork. Then, with your fingers, mix to a breadcrumb consistency.

● Knead with your hands and then form the dough into a round. Wrap with a wet cloth and leave for 30–60 minutes. Dust your worktop with flour, knead again, shape into a round and put into a strong plastic bag. Using your feet knead the dough for 10 minutes.

● Remove the dough from the bag. Dust the worktop with flour and roll the dough out to a thickness of 3–4 mm/¼ in. Dust with flour again, then fold the dough, so you can slice it easily into 5 mm/¼ in strips.

basic stocks

For many noodle dishes, a good stock is essential for success as it is the stock that imparts flavour to the dish. Basic stocks are easily prepared if somewhat time-consuming, but once the stock is prepared, noodle soups can be prepared quickly and simply. Most Asian countries have their own preferred types of stock. When you make a stock, it is wise to make more than you need at any one time as you can keep stock in the fridge for a few days, or freeze for later use. If you have no time to prepare your own stock, instant stocks are available from oriental food stockists.

chicken stock

Makes 1.75 litres/3 pt

Used to make Chinese and *Ramen* hot noodle soups and Chinese sauces. Pork bones can be replaced with more chicken bones if wished.

600 g/1¼ lb chicken bones
(such as carcasses, wings, feet
etc.), chopped roughly
100 g/4 oz pork bones
1 small onion, cut in half
20 cm/8 in leek, cut in half
diagonally
2 fat cloves garlic, crushed
2.5 cm/1 in fresh ginger, peeled
and sliced
2.25 litres/4 pt water

● Wash the bones before use. Blanch the chicken and pork bones in boiling water for 2 minutes. Rinse.
● Put the bones, onion, leek, garlic, ginger and water in a large pan. Bring to the boil, then simmer for 1 hour, skimming off the scum occasionally. After an hour, strain the stock through a very fine mesh strainer or muslin.

light chicken stock

Makes about 1.4 litres/2½ pt

Used for Thai, Malaysian and Indonesian hot noodle dishes.

1.75 litres/3 pt water
3 chicken drumsticks

● Put the water and chicken drumsticks in a saucepan, bring to the boil and simmer for about 40 minutes. When the meat on the drumstick shin begins to fall away, exposing the bone, the stock should be ready. Strain through a metal sieve and reserve the drumstick meat as a topping for a noodle dish.

miso broth

Makes 1.4 litres/2½ pt

1 tbsp sesame oil
1 cm/½ in fresh ginger, peeled
and minced
1 fat clove garlic, minced
1 spring onion, minced
4 tbsp Chinese rice wine or
Japanese *sake*
3 tbsp light soy sauce
2 tbsp caster sugar
8 tbsp red *miso* paste
2 tsp chilli oil
1.4 litres/2½ pt chicken stock
(see page 25)
black pepper

● Heat the oil in a pan. Add the ginger, garlic and spring onion and fry for 30 seconds. Add the wine first, then soy sauce, sugar, *miso* paste and chilli oil and mix together. Add the chicken stock and bring to the boil. Remove from the heat and the broth is now ready to use.

Left *Ingredients for vegetable stock*

soy sauce broth

Makes 1.4 litres/2½ pt

1.4 litres/2½ pt chicken stock
(see page 25)
2 tsp salt
4 tsp Chinese rice wine or
Japanese *sake*
2 tsp lard
4 tbsp light soy sauce
4 tsp dark soy sauce
black pepper

● Put the stock, salt, wine and lard in a pan. Bring to the boil and simmer for 2–3 minutes. Turn off the heat and add the light and dark soy sauce, black pepper and stir. It is now ready to use.

vegetable stock

Makes about 1 litre/1¾ pt

For vegetarians, vegetable stock can be substituted for chicken stock.

1 tbsp vegetable oil
1 fat clove garlic, sliced
2.5 cm/1 in fresh ginger, sliced
½ leek, sliced
50 g/2 oz carrots, chopped
1 medium-sized onion,
chopped
1½ sticks celery, chopped
1.1 litres/2 pt water

● Heat the oil in a saucepan and fry all the vegetables for 2 minutes. Add the water, bring to the boil and simmer for 40 minutes. Strain through a metal sieve.

premier Japanese dashi (stock)

Makes about 1.4 litres/2½ pt

Used for making Japanese broth.

1.4 litres/2½ pt water
10 cm/4 in dried kelp (*konbu*),
wiped with a damp cloth
50 g/2 oz bonito flakes (*katsuo-bushi*)

● First, make two or three cuts about 2.5 cm/1 in long in the kelp to release more flavour, then put the water and kelp in a saucepan and heat under a low flame. Remove the kelp just before the water begins to boil. Add the bonito flakes when the liquid comes back to the boil, and turn off the heat. Leave the liquid until the flakes sink to the bottom of the pan, then sieve through a muslin or paper filter. Retain the bonito flakes and kelp for preparing standard *dashi*.

standard Japanese dashi (stock)

Makes about 1.4 litres/2½ pt

Standard dashi recycles bonito flakes and kelp used to make Premier Japanese Dashi. It is used in the same way.

1.4 litres/2½ pt water
used kelp and bonito flakes
from premier *dashi*

● Put the water, kelp and bonito flakes in a large saucepan. Bring to the boil over a low heat and simmer for about 5 minutes. Skim off any scum that forms on the surface. Sieve through muslin or a coffee filter.

dashi broth

kake-tsuyu
Makes about 1.4 litres/2½ pt

2 tbsp *mirin*
1.4 litres/2½ pt premier *dashi*
90 ml/3½ fl oz Japanese soy
sauce
3 tbsp caster sugar

● Put the *mirin* in a saucepan and bring to the boil. Add the *dashi*, soy sauce and sugar and simmer for about 3–4 minutes. It is now ready to use.

dipping broth

tsuke-tsuyu
Makes about 750 ml/1¼ pt

150 ml/6 fl oz *mirin*
500 ml/18 fl oz premier *dashi*
150 ml/6 fl oz Japanese soy
sauce

● Put the *mirin* in a saucepan and bring to the boil. Add the *dashi* and soy sauce and simmer for 3–4 minutes, then remove from the heat and chill in the fridge.
● Dipping broth can be stored refrigerated in a jar for 3–4 days.

hot and sour noodle soup with prawns

tom yam goong with rice vermicelli

Tom yam goong is one of the representative dishes of Thai cuisine. The broth is a myriad of flavours; the sour element of lime leaves and lemon grass combined with the hot chilli pepper and *nam pla* with its strong seafood aroma.

1 tbsp vegetable oil
2 cloves garlic, grated
2 shallots, grated
2.5 cm/1 in *galangal* or ½-inch
  fresh ginger, thinly sliced
4–5 small red chillies, chopped
1.4 litres/2½ pt light chicken
  stock *(see page 25)*
3 Kaffir lime leaves, sliced
10 cm/4 in lemon grass,
  chopped
200 g/7 oz rice vermicelli
20 peeled tiger prawns
6 tbsp fish sauce (*nam pla*)
6 tbsp fresh lemon or lime juice
2 tbsp palm or brown sugar
16 tinned straw mushrooms
coriander leaves

● Heat the oil in a saucepan, stir-fry the garlic, shallots, *galangal* and chilli for about 1 minute. Put in the chicken stock, add the lime leaves and lemon grass, bring to the boil and simmer for 5 minutes.

● Meanwhile, soak the rice vermicelli for 3 minutes, rinse, drain and divide into four bowls. Add the prawns, fish sauce, lemon or lime juice, sugar and straw mushrooms to the soup and simmer for 2–3 minutes.

● Pour the soup into the bowls and sprinkle with the coriander leaves. Serve immediately.

hot and sour noodle soup with chicken

tom yam with rice vermicelli

This is another hot and sour Thai noodle soup. The authentic Thai version blends ferocious heat with refreshing sourness. I have not used as much chilli in this recipe, but I assure you it is still hot enough.

1 tbsp vegetable oil
2 cloves garlic, minced
2 shallots, minced
2.5 cm/1 in *galangal* **or ½-inch fresh ginger, thinly sliced**
5–6 small red chillies, chopped
1.4 litres/1½ pt light chicken stock *(see page 25)*
3 Kaffir lime leaves, sliced
5 cm/2 in lemon grass, sliced
200 g/7 oz rice vermicelli
6 tbsp fish sauce (*nam pla***)**
6 tbsp fresh lemon juice
2 tsp palm or brown sugar
16 tinned straw mushrooms
chicken meat from the light chicken stock, thinly sliced
1 large lettuce leaf, shredded
coriander leaves

● Heat the oil in a saucepan, stir fry the garlic, shallots, *galangal* and chilli for 2 minutes. Add the chicken stock, lime leaves and lemon grass. Bring to the boil and simmer for 5 minutes.
● Soak the rice vermicelli in warm water, rinse and drain. Put the vermicelli into four bowls. Add the fish sauce, lemon juice, sugar, straw mushrooms and chicken meat to the soup and simmer for 2–3 minutes.
● Add the lettuce and coriander and simmer for 1 minute. Pour the soup into the bowls and serve immediately.

creamy coconut noodle soup

laksa lemak

A famous Malaysian dish reflecting the multi-cultural nature of that country and its people. Laksa lemak should be treated with caution. Eaten once and you will be hopelessly addicted to its smooth texture and silky hot taste!

8 shallots, sliced
3 cloves garlic, sliced
5 cm/2 in *galangal* **or 1-inch fresh ginger, peeled and sliced**
4 small red chillies, sliced
1 tbsp chopped fresh lemon grass
5 tbsp vegetable oil
2 tsp ground turmeric
1 tsp ground coriander
2 tsp dried shrimp paste (*belacan***) (optional)**
100 g/4 oz bean curd (*tofu***), diced**
500 ml/18 fl oz light chicken stock *(see page 25)*
900 ml/1¾ pt coconut milk (tinned)
2 tsp sugar
2 tsp salt
2 fish balls, sliced
200 g/7 oz rice vermicelli
12 tiger or large prawns, peeled and deveined
For the garnish:
cooked chicken from the light chicken stock, shredded
100 g/4 oz bean sprouts
5 cm/2 in cucumber, shredded
1 large red chilli, sliced
2 spring onions, chopped

● Blend the shallots, garlic, *galangal*, red chilli and lemon grass in a mixer or food processor. Heat 3 tablespoons of the oil in a saucepan and stir-fry the shallot mixture with the turmeric, coriander and dried shrimp paste over a low heat for 3–4 minutes
● Heat the remaining oil in a frying pan and fry the bean curd until lightly browned. Add the chicken stock, coconut milk, sugar, salt and fish balls, bring to the boil and simmer for 2–3 minutes.
● Meanwhile, blanch the bean sprouts in boiling water for 1 minute. Soak the vermicelli in warm water for 3 minutes, rinse and drain well. Divide the vermicelli into four bowls.
● Add the prawns to the soup and simmer for 2 minutes. Pour the soup into the bowls, garnish with shredded chicken, bean sprouts, cucumber, sliced chilli and spring onion. Serve immediately.

Right

Creamy Coconut Noodle Soup

Malaysian sour noodle soup

laksa penang

This is a version of laksa lemak from Penang. The stock is made from fish and coconut milk is not used. The soup has a spicy, sour taste.

450 g/1 lb cod
1.6 litres/2¾ pt water
4 shallots, sliced
2 cloves garlic, sliced
5 cm/2 in *galangal* or fresh ginger, chopped
3 small red chillies, chopped
5 cm/2 in fresh lemon grass
2 tbsp vegetable oil
2 tsp ground turmeric
2 tsp dried shrimp paste (*belacan*) (optional)
4 tbsp tamarind pulp
2 tsp salt
2 tsp sugar
200 g/7 oz rice vermicelli
For the garnish:
100 g/4 oz bean sprouts
2 rings tinned pineapple, chopped
5 cm/2 in cucumber, shredded
3 fresh Kaffir lime leaves, sliced
mint leaves, sliced
1 large red chilli, sliced

● Put the cod and water in a saucepan, bring to the boil and simmer for 15–20 minutes. Meanwhile, blend the shallots, garlic, *galangal*, small red chillies and lemon grass in a mixer or food processor.

● When the fish stock is ready, take out the fish, remove the skin and flake the meat. Heat the oil in saucepan, fry the shallot mixture with the ground turmeric and dried shrimp paste for 3–4 minutes.

● Soak the tamarind pieces in warm water for 5 minutes and sieve to squeeze and extract the juice. Add the fish stock, fish flakes, salt, sugar and tamarind juice to the fried spice mixture in the pan and simmer for 3–4 minutes.

● Soak the rice vermicelli in warm water for 3 minutes, rinse and drain well. Put into four bowls. Blanch the bean sprouts in boiling water for 1 minute.

● Pour the fish soup into serving bowls. Garnish with the bean sprouts, pineapple, cucumber, lime leaves, mint leaves and red chilli. Serve at once.

Indonesian chicken soup with rice vermicelli

soto ayam

This Indonesian soup dish has a spicy, sour and nutty flavour. *Sambal oelek* provides the spice in this soup. If you like a hotter taste, simply add more. If you can not obtain galangal, substitute ginger, but use only half the amount.

2 tbsp vegetable oil
4 shallots, sliced
3 cloves garlic, sliced
5 cm/2 in *galangal* or 1-inch fresh ginger, sliced
1 tsp ground coriander
3 tbsp candle or macadamia nuts
1.4 litres/2½ pt light chicken stock (*see page 25*)
2 tsp salt
cooked chicken meat from the light chicken stock, shredded
200 g/7 oz rice vermicelli
For the topping:
2 tsp salt
100 g/4 oz bean sprouts, blanched
2 spring onions, chopped
1 stick celery, sliced
2 tbsp ready-made crispy onions
4 lime wedges
2 tsp Indonesian chilli paste (*sambal oelek*) or chilli sauce

● Heat the oil in a frying pan. Fry the shallots, garlic, *galangal* and ground coriander and add the nuts. Blend to a purée with 3 tablespoons chicken stock in a mixer or food processor.

● Put the purée and chicken stock in a pan and simmer for 5 minutes. Then add the chicken meat and salt, and simmer for 2–3 minutes. Meanwhile, soak the rice vermicelli in warm water for 3 minutes. Rinse, drain and divide into four bowls.

● Put the bean sprouts, spring onion and celery on the noodles. Pour the soup in and sprinkle over the crispy onions. Garnish with lime wedges and half a teaspoon of chilli paste to each bowl. Serve immediately.

Right
Ramen with
Wakame

ramen with wakame

Wakame seaweed is sold either dried or salted. The dried variety is more easily preserved and handled. *Wakame* is very nutritious, full of minerals and trace elements and virtually non-calorific. It makes a healthy hot noodle soup dish.

450 g/1 lb *ramen* noodles, *or*
    400 g/14 oz fresh *or* 300 g/11 oz
    dried medium egg noodles
1.4 litres/2½ pt soy sauce broth
    (see page 26)
For the topping:
2½ tbsp dried *wakame* seaweed,
    soaked in hot water and
    drained
4 tbsp cooked dried bamboo
    shoots (*shinachiku*) (optional)
2 spring onions, chopped
2 boiled eggs, cut in half

● Boil plenty of water in a pan. Add the noodles and cook for 4 minutes. Drain and put into four bowls.
● Heat the soy sauce broth. Place the *wakame*, bamboo shoots, spring onions and eggs on the noodles. Pour the soy sauce broth gently into the bowls. Serve immediately.

ramen with pork and bean curd

Pork and bean curd, called Ma Po's Tofu in China, is a popular family dish throughout east Asia. It is commonly served with rice. However, this spicy sauce with pork and bean curd really goes down just as well piled on to a bowl of hot noodles.

450 g/1 lb *ramen* noodles, *or*
    400 g/14 oz fresh *or* 300 g/
    11 oz dried thin egg noodles
1.4 litres/2½ pt soy sauce broth
    (see page 26)
2 spring onions, chopped
For the topping:
1 tbsp vegetable oil
1 fat clove garlic, minced
1 cm/½ in ginger, peeled and
    minced
150 g/6 oz minced pork
½ leek, finely sliced
300 ml/½ pt chicken stock
    (see page 25)
1 tbsp chilli bean sauce
    (*toban djan*)
2 tsp caster sugar
1 tsp light soy sauce
1 tbsp Chinese rice wine or dry
    sherry
1 tsp tomato purée
400 g/14 oz bean curd (*tofu*),
    diced
2 tbsp cornflour mixed with
    2 tbsp of water

● To make the pork with bean curd, heat the oil in a wok or frying pan until very hot. Fry the garlic and ginger for 1 minute. Then add the pork and stir-fry for 3–4 minutes.
● Add the leek and stir-fry for another minute. Then add the stock, chilli sauce, sugar, soy sauce, wine and tomato purée and bring to the boil.
● Add the bean curd and simmer for about 5–7 minutes. Next add the cornflour paste and stir to thicken.
● Boil plenty of water in a pan and add the noodles. Cook for 3 minutes and then drain. Place the noodles in individual bowls. Heat the soy broth.
● Put a quarter of the bean curd mixture and spring onions on to each serving of noodles. Gently pour the broth over. Serve at once.

ramen with garlic

Do not be surprised at the amount of garlic used in this recipe. The key point of this dish is the strong garlic flavouring which makes it a warming dish for a cold winter's day.

1 tbsp sesame oil
16 cloves garlic, sliced
450 g/1 lb *ramen* noodles, *or*
  400 g/14 oz fresh *or* 300 g/
  11 oz dried thin egg noodles
4 cloves garlic, crushed
1.4 litres/2½ pt soy sauce broth
  (see page 26)
4 tbsp cooked dried bamboo
  shoots (*shinachiku*) (optional)
2 spring onions, chopped

● Heat the sesame oil in a frying pan. Fry the garlic for 2–3 minutes or until turned golden brown. Set aside.
● Boil plenty of water in a pan and add the noodles. Cook for 3 minutes and drain. Place the noodles in individual bowls.
● Put the crushed garlic and soy sauce broth in a pan. Bring to the boil and simmer for 2–3 minutes.
● Put a quarter of the fried garlic, bamboo shoots and spring onions on to each serving of noodles. Pour the broth over the top and serve immediately.

ramen with stir-fried vegetables

Ramen noodles topped with a blend of fresh and flash-fried vegetables – deliciously simple and simply delicious!

450 g/1 lb *ramen* noodles, *or*
  400 g/14 oz fresh *or* 300 g/
  11 oz dried thin egg noodles
1.4 litres/2½ pt soy sauce broth
  (see page 26)
For the topping:
2 tbsp vegetable oil
1 tbsp sesame oil
1 small onion, sliced
80 g/3 oz mangetout, cut in half
  diagonally
50 g/2 oz carrots, cut into long
  matchsticks
200 g/7 oz bean sprouts
200 g/7 oz Chinese leaves,
  chopped
2 dried black ear fungi or dried
  shiitaki mushrooms, soaked in
  water, rinsed and chopped
salt and pepper

● Heat the oils in a wok or frying pan until very hot. Stir-fry the onion, mangetout and carrots for 2 minutes, then add the bean sprouts, Chinese leaves, black fungi and stir-fry for another 3–4 minutes. Season with salt and pepper.
● Boil plenty of water in a large pan and add the noodles. Cook for 3 minutes before draining well. Put the noodles into four bowls.
● Heat the soy sauce broth. Pile the stir-fried vegetables on to the noodles and pour the broth over. Serve at once.

Right
*Ramen with
Stir-fried
Vegetables*

ramen with chicken nuggets

Deep-fried, spicy chicken nuggets are a favourite in Japan, served on their own or as an accompaniment to a dish, such as below, which should fill even the emptiest stomach.

450 g/1 lb *ramen* noodles, or
400 g/14 oz fresh or 300 g/
11 oz dried thin egg noodles
1.4 litres/2½ pt soy sauce broth
(see page 26)
4 tbsp cooked dried bamboo
shoots (*shinachiku*) (optional)
watercress for garnish
For the nuggets:
black pepper
2 boneless chicken breasts,
roughly diced
3 tbsp soy sauce
vegetable oil for deep frying
2 tbsp cornflour
2 tbsp plain flour
½ tbsp garlic powder
½ tbsp ginger powder

● Sprinkle the black pepper over the chicken and marinate with the soy sauce for 30 minutes. Heat the oil to 180°C/350°F in a saucepan. Mix the cornflour, plain flour, garlic powder and ginger powder together in a bowl. Coat the chicken with the flour mixture and deep fry until golden brown.
● Boil plenty of water in a pan and boil the noodles for 3 minutes or according to the instructions on the packet. Drain and put into four bowls.
● Heat the soy sauce broth. Place the chicken nuggets, bamboo shoots and watercress on the noodles. Pour the broth over and serve at once.

ramen with barbecued pork

cha siu mein

Cha siu is a spicy Chinese marinade and cha siu pork is widely eaten all over south-east Asia. *Cha siu* pork is roasted for a comparatively short time compared to roast pork dishes prepared in the West. *Cha siu* sauce is available from Chinese stores and bigger supermarkets.

450 g/1 lb *ramen* noodles, or
400 g/14 oz fresh or 300 g/
11 oz dried thin egg noodles
1.4 litres/2½ pt soy sauce broth
(see page 26)
For the topping:
12 large slices Chinese style
barbecued pork (*cha siu*)
4 tbsp cooked dried bamboo
shoots (*shinachiku*) (optional)
3 spring onions, chopped

● Boil plenty of water in a pan and cook the noodles for 3 minutes. Drain and divide into four bowls. Heat the soy sauce broth.
● Put three slices of *cha siu* into each bowl of noodles. Garnish with the bamboo shoots and spring onions. Pour the soy sauce broth over just before serving.

How to make *cha siu* pork

900 g/2 lb pork tenderloin
8 tbsp *cha siu* sauce for
marinating

Marinate the pork in the *cha siu* sauce for at least an hour or preferably 3–4 hours. Preheat the oven to 190°C/375°F/Gas Mark 5. Place the pork on a rack on a baking tray lined with aluminium foil. Bake for 60–70 minutes, basting a few times. The outside of the pork should be browned and the inside still tender.

Right
Ramen with Barbecued Pork

ramen with crab omelette

kanitama-ramen

Typically, crab omelette is served on its own. The inspiration behind the dish is Chinese but the Japanese have a preference for it served on a bowl of noodles. Ideally, individual omelettes for each person should be made, but if time is against you, make one large one and cut it into four.

450 g/1 lb *ramen* noodles, or
  400 g/14 oz fresh or 300 g/
  11 oz dried thin egg noodles
1.4 litres/2½ pt soy sauce broth
  (see page 26)
For the omelette:
6 eggs
150 g/6 oz crab meat (tinned)
4 *shiitake* mushrooms, sliced
2 spring onions, thinly sliced
4 tbsp tinned bamboo shoots,
  thinly sliced
salt and white pepper
2–3 tbsp vegetable oil
1 spring onion, chopped

● First, to make the omelette, put the eggs, crab meat, mushrooms, spring onions and bamboo shoots in a bowl. Season with salt and pepper, and mix.

● Heat the oil in a frying pan or wok until very hot. Pour in the egg mixture and heat for 30 seconds. Stir lightly with chopsticks or a spatula a few times. When it is nearly set, turn it over. The mixture should be soft like scrambled egg, but be cooked just enough to be able to retain the shape of an omelette.

● Boil plenty of water in a large pan. Add the noodles and cook for 3 minutes, or according to the instructions on the packet. Drain and divide into four bowls.

● Heat the soy sauce broth. Place the crab omelette on the noodles and pour the broth over. Sprinkle the spring onion and serve immediately.

ramen with wontons

Wontons, spicy parcels of minced pork, are another Chinese creation which has been exported far and wide. Wonton wrappers are available from oriental food stores and can be frozen. Slippery little creatures that they are, wonton parcels served in a bowl of noodles demand good chopstick technique if a humiliating resort to a spoon is to be avoided!

300 g/11 oz *ramen* or fresh thin
  egg noodles
1.4 litres/2½ pt soy sauce broth
  (see page 26)
2 large lettuce leaves, blanched
3 spring onions, chopped
For the wontons:
80 g/3 oz minced pork
1 spring onion, minced
1 dried *shiitake* mushroom,
  soaked in hot water, then
  minced
5 mm/¼ in fresh ginger, peeled
  and sliced
½ tsp light soy sauce
¼ tsp Chinese rice wine or dry
  sherry
¼ tsp sesame oil
salt
20 wonton wrappers

● Mix the minced pork, spring onion, *shiitake* mushroom, ginger, soy sauce, rice wine, sesame oil and salt together in a bowl. Take 1 tsp of the meat mixture and put it on the centre of a wonton wrapper. Wet the edge with water and fold over into a clam shape. Seal the edge well, taking care to press out any air caught inside the wonton. Next draw the two ends, wet one side with water and pinch together. Make the rest of the wontons in the same way.

● Bring water in two saucepans to the boil. Cook the noodles for 3 minutes in one of them, and boil the wontons for about 3–4 minutes in the other saucepan. Drain the noodles and wontons well. First, divide the noodles into four bowls, then put the wontons on the noodles.

● Heat the soy sauce broth. Place the blanched lettuce and spring onions on the noodles. Pour the broth over and serve at once.

Right
Ramen with
Crab
Omelette

ramen with sweetcorn and butter

This dish is universally popular as a lunch dish or light meal and melted butter and sweetcorn are particular favourites with the Japanese.

450 g/1 lb fresh *ramen* noodles
1.4 litres/2½ pt chicken stock
(see page 25)
6 tbsp Japanese soy sauce
1 tsp salt
a pinch of freshly ground black
pepper
For the topping:
16 tbsp tinned sweetcorn
kernels
6 spring onions, chopped
40 g/1½ oz butter, sliced into
four pieces

● Boil the noodles for about 2–2½ minutes. Drain and put them in individual bowls.

● Boil the stock, soy sauce, salt and pepper in a pan. When it boils, pour the soup into the bowls. Put 4 tablespoons of the sweetcorn each on top of the noodles, sprinkle with the chopped spring onion, then top with the butter. Eat as soon as possible or the noodles will absorb the soup and become soggy.

miso ramen with sweetcorn

The *miso* broth used in this dish has a sweet, spicy flavour. The taste of the broth will different depending on the variety of *miso* used. Once you have prepared the tasty broth, this simple and quick *ramen* dish is ready to eat in minutes. For an easy variation, try a knob of butter dropped on to the noodles to enrich the taste.

450 g/1 lb *ramen* noodles, *or*
400 g/14 oz fresh *or* 300 g/
11 oz dried thin egg noodles
1.4 litres/2½ pt *miso* broth
(see page 25)
For the topping:
16 tbsp tinned sweetcorn
½ punnet cress
3 spring onions, chopped
½ sheet *nori* seaweed, cut in
four

● Boil plenty of water in a pan. Add the noodles and cook for 3 minutes. Drain and divide into individual bowls.
● Heat the *miso* broth. Pile the sweetcorn on to the noodles and then the cress, spring onions and *nori*. Gently pour the *miso* broth over and serve at once.

miso ramen with bean sprouts

In this recipe, medium egg noodles are used but thin egg noodles can be used in their place if wished. When you blanch the bean sprouts take care not to overcook them. They should still be crispy when eaten.

400 g/14 oz bean sprouts
450 g/1 lb *ramen* noodles, *or*
400 g/14 oz fresh *or* 300 g/
11 oz dried thin egg noodles
1.4 litres/2½ pt *miso* broth
(see page 25)
½ sheet *nori* seaweed, cut into
four
½ punnet cress

● Boil the water in a pan and blanch the bean sprouts for 30 seconds. Drain.
● Boil plenty of water in a pan and add the noodles. Cook for 3 minutes and drain. Place the noodles in individual bowls.
● Heat the *miso* broth. Put a quarter of the bean sprouts, a square of *nori* and some cress on to each serving of noodles and pour the *miso* broth over. Serve immediately.

Right

Buckwheat
Noodles
with a King
Prawn

buckwheat noodles with a king prawn

Topping a dish of *soba* noodles with a king prawn turns a nourishing meal into a gourmet experience.

4 king or tiger prawns
a little plain flour
8 shiitake mushrooms
400 g/14 oz dried *soba*
For the batter:
4 tbsp plain flour
1 egg, beaten
8 tbsp water
For the soup:
1.4 litres/2½ pt dashi broth
  (see page 26)

● To make the topping mix the flour, egg and water lightly in a bowl. Coat the prawns with flour and dip in the batter. Dip the mushrooms into the batter. Heat the oil to 180°C/350°F and deep fry until golden brown.
● Bring a large pan of water to the boil. Add the *soba* and cook for about 5 minutes. Briefly rinse with cold water and then drain. Divide the *soba* equally between four bowls.
● Bring the Dashi Broth to the boil in a saucepan. Add to the bowls of *soba*.
● Place one prawn and two mushrooms on the top of each bowl. Serve immediately.

miso ramen with shredded leek

Noodles in *miso* broth are one of the most popular noodle dishes served in Japan. It is essential to use a good quality *miso* paste as this provides the crucial sweet and salty flavouring to the dish. The shredded leek should have a firm, supple texture, so if prepared beforehand, soak in a little water to prevent it from drying out.

200 g/7 oz fresh spinach
450 g/1 lb *ramen* noodles, or
  400 g/14 oz fresh *or* 300 g/
  11 oz dried egg noodles
1.4 litres/2½ pt *miso* broth
  (see page 25)
10 cm/4 in leek, cut in four
  pieces and shredded
4 tbsp cooked dried bamboo
  shoots (*shinachiku*) (optional)

● Bring some water to the boil in a pan and blanch the spinach for 1–2 minutes. Rinse, drain and divide into four equal portions.
● Bring more water to the boil in a large saucepan. Add the noodles and boil for 4 minutes. Drain and place into individual serving bowls.
● Heat the *miso* broth for 2–3 minutes. Pile the leek, spinach and bamboo shoots on top of the noodles. Add the miso broth. Serve immediately.

Right

Miso
Ramen
with
Shredded
Leek

egg noodle soup with pork chop

You would be hard pressed to find a better way of serving pork chops than with the fiery, sweet marinade used here. Strictly speaking, Chinese rice wine should be used in this dish but I have found that a dry sherry can be used as a substitute without any drastic change in flavour.

4 pork chops, off the bone and lightly tenderized
1.4 litres/2½ pt chicken stock
  (see page 25)
1 tbsp Chinese rice wine or dry sherry
2 tsp salt
white pepper
2 lettuce leaves, quartered
4–5 tbsp vegetable oil
450 g/1 lb *ramen* noodles, *or* 400 g/14 oz fresh *or* 300 g/ 11 oz dried medium egg noodles
For the marinade:
1 clove garlic, minced
1 spring onion, chopped
1 tbsp light soy sauce
1 tbsp dark soy sauce
2 tbsp Chinese rice wine or dry sherry
1 tbsp caster sugar
a pinch of pepper
2 tsp cornflour

● Mix the garlic, spring onion, soy sauce, rice wine, sugar, pepper and cornflour together, then marinate the pork chops for 30 minutes.

● Meanwhile, put the chicken stock, rice wine, salt and pepper in a pan. Bring to the boil and simmer for 3 minutes. Blanch the lettuce leaves in a pan for 1 minute. Set aside.

● Heat the oil in a wok or frying pan. Shallow fry the pork chops for 2–3 minutes on each side until lightly browned. (Frying time will vary with the thickness of the pork.) Cut into strips 2.5 cm/1 in wide.

● Bring plenty of water to the boil in a large pan and add the egg noodles. Cook for 4 minutes or according to the instructions on the packet. Drain well and put into four bowls.

● Place the pork and lettuce leaves on the noodles and pour the hot broth over. Serve immediately.

udon noodles with egg

kakitama-udon

Udon is a great favourite in the winter months because of its warming properties. *Udon* comes in various shapes, some flat, some round in section, some as thick as a little finger, others as thin as spaghetti.

600 g/1¼ lb parboiled fresh *udon*
1.4 litres/2½ pt *dashi* broth
   (see page 26)
2 eggs, beaten
4 tsp cornflour
4 tsp water
4 spring onions, chopped

● Bring a large pan of water to the boil. Add the *udon* and boil for 3 minutes. Drain and then place in equal portions into the four bowls.

● Bring the Dashi Broth to the boil in a saucepan. Pour ⅔ of the liquid into the 4 bowls. Bring the remainder back to the boil and gradually add the egg, mixing lightly so that when the egg rises to the surface, it is cooked in fronds.

● Mix the cornflour and water into a paste and then add this to the soup to thicken. Pour the egg mixture into the bowls. Sprinkle with the spring onion and serve immediately.

egg noodle soup with spicy sesame sauce

dan dan mian

This is a famous Sichuan dish although it has gained popularity in other Asian countries. There are several versions to this recipe, but all include the rich aromatic sesame sauce which gives full flavour to the soup. You can adjust the amount of chilli oil to your liking.

450 g/1 lb *ramen* noodles, or
   400 g/14 oz fresh or 300 g/
   11 oz dried thin egg noodles
1.25 litres/2¼ pt chicken stock
   (see page 25)
For the spicy sesame sauce:
1 tbsp vegetable oil
2.5 cm/1 in fresh ginger, peeled
   and minced
3 cloves garlic, minced
225 g/8 oz pork, minced
8 *shiitake* mushrooms, finely
   chopped
4 spring onions, finely chopped
6 tbsp sesame sauce
5 tbsp light soy sauce
1 tbsp chilli oil

● First, to make the spicy sesame sauce, heat the oil in a frying pan. Fry the ginger and garlic for 30 seconds, add the pork, mushrooms and spring onions, and stir fry for 3–4 minutes.

● Add the sesame sauce, soy sauce, chilli oil and stir for 1–2 minutes. Set aside.

● Boil plenty of water in a pan, add the noodles and cook for about 3 minutes or according to the instructions on the packet. Drain and divide into four bowls.

● Heat the chicken stock. Pour the spicy sesame sauce over the noodles. Gently pour the stock into the bowls. Serve at once.

sukiyaki udon

Sukiyaki itself is a famous Japanese dish. *Udon* are often combined with sukiyaki in Japanese homes, stirred in alongside the steak and vegetables and left to cook and absorb all the delicious flavours cooking away in the pot.

150 ml/¼ pt premier *dashi*
  (see page 26)
1½ tbsp sugar
2 tbsp sake
2½ tbsp soy sauce
2 spring onions, chopped
225 g/8 oz rump steak, thinly
  sliced in 2-in strips
½ leek, sliced diagonally
4 Chinese leaves, diced
4 *shiitake* mushrooms, halved
600 g/1¼ lb parboiled fresh *udon*
1.4 litres/2½ pt *dashi* broth
  (see page 26)

To make the sukiyaki:
● Put the dashi, sugar, sake and soy sauce into a pan and bring to the boil. Add the steak, leek, Chinese leaves and *shiitake*, then simmer for 7–10 minutes. Set aside.
● Boil plenty of water in a pan. Add the *udon* and boil for 3 minutes. Drain and rinse with cold water. Drain again and divide into four bowls.
● Heat the broth. Place the sukiyaki on top of the noodles and pour the broth over the top. Serve immediately.

udon with bean curd sheet
kitsune udon

Abura-age are deep-fried sheets of tofu, available at most stores which stock Japanese foodstuffs. They can be stored at home in the freezer but will quickly go off if left for any time in the refrigerator.

600 g/1¼ lb parboiled fresh
  udon
1.4 litres/2½ pt *dashi* broth
  (see page 26)
For the topping:
4 bean curd sheets (*abura-age*),
  cut into halves
200 ml/7 fl oz premier *dashi*
  (see page 26)
2 tbsp caster sugar
2½ tbsp soy sauce
225 g/8 oz fresh spinach
2 spring onions, chopped
a pinch of salt
seven flavours chilli powder
  (*shichimi*) (optional)

● Rinse the *abura-age* in hot water. Put it into a saucepan of boiling water together with the *dashi,* sugar and soy sauce. Simmer for about 20 minutes or until the fluid has reduced to third.
● Bring plenty of water to boil in a pan and add the *udon*. Cook for 3 minutes. Drain and rinse with cold water, then drain once more. Divide and put into individual serving bowls.
● Blanch the spinach in boiling water for 1 minute, then drain and squeeze out the excess water. Heat the *dashi* broth.
● Put two half sheets of *abura-age*, some spinach and spring onions on to each serving of *udon*. Pour the broth over the top, sprinkle with the seven flavours chilli powder and serve.

udon with egg strands

tamago-toji udon

The addition of beaten egg to a bowl of *udon* enriches the noodles and thickens the broth while retaining the essential lightness of the dish. The strands of egg are easy to make as long as the beaten egg is dribbled into the broth, not added all at once. For the best result, do as I have done here, and beat the strands into individual portion of broth.

600 g/1¼ lb parboiled fresh udon
1.4 litres/2½ pt dashi broth
 (see page 26)
3 eggs, beaten
watercress for garnish

● Bring plenty of water to boil in a pan and add the *udon*. Cook for 3 minutes. Drain and rinse with cold water. Drain once more. Divide and place in individual serving bowls.

● Bring the *dashi* broth to the boil and pour one quarter into a sauce-pan. To make the "egg flowers", dribble a quarter of the beaten egg into the saucepan, stirring occasionally with a chopstick or similar to pull out the strands. Repeat three more times. Pour the egg strand broth on to the noodles, garnish with the cress and serve immediately.

udon with five toppings

okame udon

A filling dish of *udon* with several toppings. To make the Japanese-style omelette successfully a non-stick pan is essential. If you can't find a shop that stocks Japanese fish cake, or *kamaboko*, seafood sticks can be pressed into service in their place.

600 g/1¼ lb parboiled fresh udon
1.4 litres/2½ pt dashi broth
 (see page 26)
For the topping
4 shiitake mushrooms
300 ml/11 fl oz dashi (see page 26)
2½ tbsp soy sauce
2½ tbsp mirin
225 g/8 oz fresh spinach
4 slices Japanese fishcake
 (kamaboko) or seafood sticks
½ punnet cress
For the omelettes:
2 eggs
2 tsp mirin
¼ tsp soy sauce
a pinch of salt
2 tsp vegetable oil

● Put the *shiitake*, *dashi*, soy sauce and mirin into a saucepan, bring to the boil and simmer for 8–10 minutes before setting aside. Discard the liquid when the *shiitake* are ready to be added to the *udon*.

● To make the egg omelette, beat the eggs, mirin, soy sauce and salt together in a bowl. Heat the oil in a frying pan. Pour a third of the egg mixture into the pan. When it is half set, gently roll it up and over to one side of the pan. Add another third of the mixture. Wait until this has half set, roll the first third over to the other side of the pan so it picks up the second third as it

goes. Repeat once more before leaving to cool. When cooled, cut into eight pieces.

● Cook the spinach in boiling water for 1–2 minutes. Rinse with cold water and squeeze out. Cut into four portions.

● Cook the *udon* in a saucepan of boiling water for about three minutes. Rinse, drain and divide equally into four bowls.

● Heat the *dashi* broth. Put one *shiitake* mushroom, 2 slices of omelette, 1 portion of spinach, 1 slice of fish cake and a quarter of the cress into each bowl. Pour the hot *dashi* broth over the top and serve immediately.

Left

Udon with

Five

Toppings

kishimen udon

Kishimen is a flat Japanese variation on *udon*, not unlike Chinese rick stick noodles, or Italian fettucine if you prefer a European analogy. The recipe below pairs them with a light and nutritious combination of fresh vegetables and seafood.

600 g/1¼ lb parboiled fresh
    kishimen* or *udon
1.4 litres/2½ pt *dashi* broth
    (*see page 26*)
For the topping:
8 mangetout
8 seafood sticks
½ sheet *nori* seaweed, cut into
    four strips
4 spring onions, chopped

● Cook the mangetout in a pan of boiling water for 2 minutes. Rinse with cold water and set aside.

● Bring plenty of water to the boil in a saucepan and add the noodles. Boil for 3 minutes then drain and rinse with cold water. Drain again and then divide into four serving bowls.

● Place 2 mangetout, 2 seafood sticks, 1 strip of *nori* and a quarter of the spring onions on top of each serving. Heat the *dashi* broth and pour into the bowls. Serve immediately.

udon with pork

butaniku iri udon

A deceptively simple, wholesome dish with its origin in the Japanese peasantry. You might find it hard to believe that something so simple to prepare could taste so good.

1.4 litres/2½ pt *dashi* broth
    (*see page 26*)
225 g/8 oz lean pork, thinly
    sliced on a slant into bite-sized
    pieces
1 leek, sliced diagonally
1 packet *shimeji* (or *shiitake*)
    mushrooms
600 g/1¼ lb parboiled fresh *udon*
2 eggs, beaten
2 spring onions, chopped
seven flavour chilli powder
    (shichimi) (optional)

● Bring the broth to the boil in a pan, then add the pork, leek and mushrooms and simmer for about 5 minutes until the leek has softened.

● Add the *udon* and simmer for 3 minutes. When the broth comes to the boil, pour in the beaten egg and wait for it to firm. Pile the mixture into bowls, sprinkle over the *shichimi* and serve immediately.

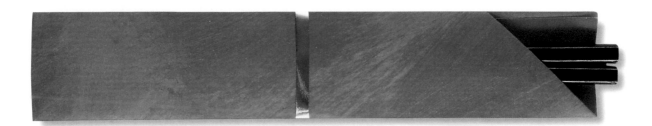

udon with curry sauce

kare udon

A modern Japanese innovation combining the spicy flavour of a curry sauce with the smooth texture of *udon* noodles.

600 g/1¼ lb parboiled fresh *udon*
1.4 litres/2½ pt *dashi* broth
  (see page 26)
For the curry:
2 tbsp vegetable oil
2 boneless chicken breasts,
  diced
1 medium-sized onion, sliced
2 tbsp plain flour
1–2 tsp curry powder
½ chicken stock cube
300 ml/11 fl oz water
2 tbsp chutney
50 g/2 oz currants
salt and pepper

● Heat the oil in a pan. Fry the chicken for 5 minutes or until cooked through. Set aside.
● Add the onion and fry until lightly browned. Add the flour and curry powder and fry for 1–2 minutes.
● Gradually dissolve the chicken stock into the water, add the chutney and currants and season with salt and pepper. Simmer for ten minutes, then stir in the cooked chicken.
● Bring plenty of water to the boil in a pan and add the *udon*. Cook for 3 minutes and drain. Rinse under cold water and drain again. Divide into serving bowls.
● Meanwhile, heat the broth. Pour the curry sauce over the *udon* and pour the broth over the top. Serve immediately.

Right *Udon with Curry Sauce*

wakame udon

A tasty and filling dish full of sea-sourced protein and minerals from *wakame* seaweed and Japanese fish cake.

600 g/1¼ lb parboiled fresh *udon*
1.4 litres/2½ pt *dashi* broth
  (see page 26)
For the topping:
4 tbsp bamboo shoots (tinned)
150 ml/¼ pt premier *dashi*
  (see page 26)
1 tbsp soy sauce
1 tbsp mirin
4 tsp dried *wakame* seaweed
8 slices Japanese fish cake
  (*kamaboko*), or seafood sticks
3 spring onions, chopped
seven flavour chilli powder
  (*shichimi*) (optional)

● Put the bamboo shoots, *dashi*, soy sauce and mirin into a pan and simmer for 7–10 minutes. Set aside.
● Bring plenty of water to the boil in a pan and add the *udon*. Cook for 3 minutes and drain. Rinse with cold water and drain again. Divide into four bowls.
● Heat the *dashi* broth. Put a quarter of the bamboo shoots, 1 tsp *wakame*, 2 slices of fish cake and a quarter of the spring onions into each bowl. Pour the hot broth over, sprinkle with *shichimi* and serve immediately.

udon hot pot

nabe-yaki udon

This dish is ideally prepared in individual clay pots and served straight from the stove. If you don't have any suitable pots, use a large stew pot or pan with a lid and divide into four serving bowls.

vegetable oil for deep frying
5 tbsp plain flour
½ egg, beaten
125 ml/4 fl oz cold water
4 king or large prawns, peeled
1.6 litres/2¾ pt *dashi* broth
  (see page 26)
600 g/1¼ lb parboiled fresh *udon*
8 shiitake mushrooms
1 packet *enoki* mushrooms or 8
  button mushrooms
½ leek, sliced diagonally
8 mangetout
4 spring onions
4 eggs

● Fill a pan one third full of oil and heat to 180°C/350°F. Mix 4 tablespoons of the flour, the beaten egg and water lightly in a bowl to make the batter. Dust the prawns with the remaining flour and dip into the batter. Deep fry in the oil until golden and crisp. Set aside.
● Heat the *dashi* broth in a pan. Add the *udon* and place the mushrooms, leek, mangetout and spring onions on top. Cover and cook for 3 minutes. Add the prawns and eggs, cover and simmer.
● When the surface of the eggs turn white, the dish is ready to serve.

miso udon hot pot

If you use dried *udon*, boil it *al dente* first. You can skip the chicken and make vegetarian hot pot, if you wish. *Gobo*, a fibrous root vegetable, is available from Japanese grocers.

1.75 litres/3 pt premier *dashi*
  (see page 26)
225 g/8 oz boneless chicken
  breasts, diced
80 g/3 oz carrots, sliced
150 g/6 oz swede, sliced into
  bite-sized pieces
½ leek, sliced diagonally
2 tbsp Japanese rice wine (*sake*)
50 g/2 oz *shimeji* mushrooms or
  8 shiitake mushrooms
30 g/1 oz *gobo* (optional), thinly
  sliced
600 g/1¼ lb parboiled fresh
  udon, rinsed
8 tbsp *miso* paste

● Put the *dashi*, chicken, carrots, swede and leek in a saucepan, bring to the boil, and then add the *sake*, mushrooms and *gobo* (if using). Simmer for 10–12 minutes.
● Add the *udon* and cook for 3 minutes. Stir in the *miso* paste. When it comes back to the boil, it is ready to serve.

udon vegetable hot pot

kenchin udon

Kenchin jiru is a vegetable stew, originally prepared for Buddhist monks. It is a very simple and delicate dish as only vegetables are used, but it will without doubt warm you up on a cold winter's day. This recipe includes several vegetables which may be unfamiliar – they are described in the glossary and are available from Japanese grocers.

2 tbsp sesame oil
150 g/6 oz carrots, cut at
 random into bite-sized pieces
150 g/6 oz mooli (*daikon*),
 quartered and sliced
280 g/10 oz *satoimo* or new
 potatoes, diced
30 g/1 oz *gobo* (optional), thinly
 sliced diagonally
150 g/6 oz bean curd (*tofu*),
 diced
1.75 litres/3 pt premier *dashi*
 (see page 26)
2 tbsp Japanese rice wine (*sake*)
2 tsp granulated sugar
2 tsp salt
3 tbsp Japanese soy sauce
600 g/1¼ lb parboiled fresh
 udon, rinsed
3 spring onions, chopped

● Heat the sesame oil in a saucepan. Stir fry the carrots, *mooli, satoimo* and *gobo* for 2 minutes. Then add the bean curd and stir.
● Add the *dashi* and *sake* and bring to the boil. Add the sugar, salt and soy sauce and simmer for 8–10 minutes.
● Add the *udon* and spring onion and simmer for a further 3 minutes. Serve immediately.

soba with egg

tsukimi soba

This dish draws its name from the egg yolk which tops it off and is said to resemble the full moon (*tsukimi* means "moon-watching" in Japanese).

380 g/13 oz *or* 400 g/14 oz dried
 soba
1.4 litres/2½ pt *dashi* broth
 (see page 26)
4 egg yolks
2 sheets of *nori* seaweed,
 shredded
½ punnet cress

● Bring plenty of water to the boil in a large pan and add the *soba*. Cook for 5–6 minutes. Drain and rinse well under cold water. Drain again. Divide into individual bowls.
● Bring the *dashi* broth to the boil and pour into each bowl.
● Place an egg yolk in the centre of each bowl and sprinkle the *nori* and cress around the egg. Serve immediately.

soba with grated yam

yamakake soba

The *yama-imo* or mountain potato is a Japanese member of the yam family. *Yama-imo* can be eaten as here, grated into a thick, spongy topping. Japanese *yama-imo*, which tends not to discolour so quickly when peeled, is recommended for this dish.

400 g/14 oz dried *soba*
1.4 litres/2½ pt *dashi* broth
 (see page 26)
For the topping:
300 g/11 oz yam (*yama-imo*)
4 quails eggs
1 sheet of *nori* seaweed,
 shredded
3 spring onions, chopped
2 tsp *wasabi* mustard (optional)

● Heat the *dashi* broth.
● Bring plenty of water to the boil in a large pan and add the *soba*. Cook for 5–6 minutes. Drain and rinse well under cold water. Drain again. Divide into serving bowls.
● Grate the yam peeling it as you go to stop it from slipping out of your fingers.
● Put the grated yam over the *soba*, then break the eggs into the centre of the grated yam. Sprinkle with *nori* and spring onion. Put a ½ teaspoon of *wasabi* at the edge of each bowl.
● Gently pour the *dashi* over and serve immediately.

Right
Soba with Grated Yam

soba with batter

tanuki soba

This dish is usually named because the *tanuki*, or badger, is reputed to have a fondness for the small droplets of batter used to top the noodles. The batter is the same type as used to make tempura, so any leftovers can be gainfully put to use.

400 g/14 oz dried *soba*
1.4 litres/2½ pt *dashi* broth
  (see *page 26*)
For the topping:
vegetable oil for frying
4 tbsp plain flour
½ egg, beaten
130 ml/4½ fl oz water
8 mangetout
3 spring onions, chopped

● Bring plenty of water to the boil in a large pan and add the *soba*. Cook for 5–6 minutes. Drain and rinse well under cold water. Drain again. Divide into serving bowls.
● To make the topping, heat the oil at 180°C/350°F in a pan. Mix the flour, egg and water lightly in a bowl. Using chopsticks, drip the mixture into the oil a little at a time, trying to avoid making big lumps of batter. When the batter has turned golden brown and floats to the surface, it is ready. Drain on absorbent paper.
● Meanwhile, blanch the mangetout for 2 minutes, rinse with cold water and drain.
● Heat the *dashi* broth.
● Place 2 tablespoonfuls of the batter in the centre of each bowl, on top of the noodles. Place 2 mangetout on top and sprinkle over the spring onion. Pour over the *dashi* broth gently and serve immediately.

soba with three mushrooms

The Japanese have a great fondness for mushrooms. This dish combines three varieties, each with its own particular shape, texture and flavour. If *shimeji* or *enoki* mushrooms are unavailable, ordinary button mushrooms or oyster mushrooms can be used instead.

400 g/14 oz dried *soba*
1.4 litres/2½ pt *dashi* broth
  (see *page 26*)
For the topping:
300 ml/11 fl oz *premier dashi*
  (see *page 26*)
1 tbsp mirin
2 tbsp soy sauce
1 tbsp caster sugar
8 *shiitake* mushrooms
1 punnet (100 g) fresh *shimeji* mushrooms, the bottom of the roots cut off
1 punnet (200 g) fresh *enoki* mushrooms, the bottom of the roots cut off
225 g/8 oz fresh spinach

● Put the *dashi*, mirin, soy sauce and sugar in a saucepan. Bring to the boil, then add the *shiitake* and *shimeji* mushrooms and simmer for 4–5 minutes. Add the *enoki* mushrooms and simmer for a further 2–3 minutes.
● Blanch the spinach in boiling water for 1–2 minutes. Rinse under water and squeeze out any excess water. Boil plenty of water in a pan and cook the *soba* for 5–6 minutes or according to the instruction on the packet. Rinse under water, drain and divide into four bowls.
● Heat the *dashi* broth. Arrange the mushrooms and spinach on the *soba*. Pour the *dashi* broth over. Serve immediately.

soba with chicken

tori-nanban

The chicken used in this dish should be marinated for as long as possible to extract as much flavour from the sauce as possible, so don't be tempted to cut down on the times below, which should be treated as a minimum.

400 g/14 oz dried *soba*
1.4 litres/2½ pt *dashi* broth
  (see *page 26*)
For the topping:
3 boneless chicken breasts, sliced on a slant into bite-sized pieces
2 tbsp Japanese soy sauce
1 leek, thinly sliced diagonally
seven flavours chilli powder (*shichimi*) (optional)
cress for garnish

● Marinate the chicken in the soy sauce for at least 15 minutes. Put the chicken, leek and *dashi* broth in a saucepan, bring to the boil and simmer for 10–15 minutes or until the chicken is cooked. Occasionally skim off the scum.
● Boil plenty of water in a large pan and add the soba. Cook for 5–6 minutes. Rinse well under water and drain thoroughly. Divide the *soba* into four bowls.
● Pour the broth with chicken and leek into the bowls. Garnish with the cress. Sprinkle with *shichimi* and serve at once.

Right

Soba with

Chicken

soba with simmered herring

nishin soba

In Japan, this dish requires the use of a kind of smoked herring not usually available overseas. For this recipe, I have found that kippers make an excellent substitute.

400 g/14 oz dried *soba*
1.4 litres/2½ pt *dashi* broth
  (*see page 26*)
For the topping:
4 kipper fillets
2 tbsp soy sauce
2 tbsp mirin
2 tbsp caster sugar
100 ml/4 fl oz water
3 spring onions, chopped
seven flavour chilli powder
  (***shichimi*) (optional)**

● Rinse the kippers in hot water. Put them, together with the soy sauce, mirin, sugar and water into a pan and simmer for about 20 minutes or until the sauce has thickened.
● Bring plenty of water to boil in a pan and add the *soba*. Cook for 5–6 minutes. Drain and rinse well under cold water. Drain again. Divide into serving bowls.
● Heat the *dashi* broth.
● Place a kipper fillet on to each serving of *soba* and sprinkle with chopped spring onion. Pour the broth over the top, sprinkle with *shichimi* and serve immediately.

soba with deep-fried king prawns

tempura soba

A dish of contrasts: the light, subtle taste of the *dashi* broth set against the richness of the deep fried prawns. Expensive as they are, try to get prawns of a decent size as they will shrink during cooking.

400 g/14 oz dried *soba*
1.4 litres/2½ pt *dashi* broth
  (*see page 26*)
For the topping:
vegetable oil for deep frying
8 king or large prawns with
  tails, peeled
9 tbsp plain flour
1 egg, beaten
225 ml/8 fl oz cold water
2 spring onions, chopped
seven flavours chilli powder
  (***shichimi*), (optional)**

● Fill a pan one third full with the oil and heat to 180°C/350°F. Mix 8 tablespoons of the flour, egg and water lightly. Coat the prawns with the remaining flour, then dip into the batter. Deep fry until golden brown. Drain on absorbent paper.
● Boil plenty of water in a pan and add the *soba*. Cook for 5–6 minutes. Rinse with water and drain. Divide into four bowls.
● Heat the *dashi* broth. Place two prawns on each serving of *soba* and sprinkle over the spring onions. Pour the *dashi* broth over, sprinkle with *shichimi* and serve at once.

Right

Soba with Simmered Herring

chilled egg noodles with tuna, prawns,
   wakame and sesame sauce

chilled egg noodles with chicken and
   pepperoni

chilled egg noodles with mackerel and
   prawns

chilled egg noodles with chicken and
   peanut sauce

chilled *udon* with five toppings

chilled *udon* with fermented soya beans

chilled *udon* with aubergine and *miso* sauce

chilled *soba* with *nameko* mushrooms

chilled *soba* with bean curd sheet

chilled *soba* with sour plum sauce

chilled *soba* with deep-fried mackerel

chilled *soba* with shredded *daikon*

chilled *soba* with deep-fried vegetables

classic cold *somen*

chilled soba with vegetable tempura

chilled *somen* with sesame dipping

chilled *somen* with pork

bean thread noodle salad with
   barbecued pork

bean thread noodle salad with prawns

cold noodle dishes

Noodles are even eaten on humid summer days in south-east Asia, when bowls of noodles are converted into cold dishes. Simple cold soba *and* somen *dishes are very popular and low in calories. Egg noodles served in a tasty sauce are irresistible and there are some tasty noodle salads.*

chilled egg noodles with tuna, prawn, wakame and sesame sauce

Noodles are just as delicious served cold as they are hot. Because they still tend to dry quickly, it is important to eat them as soon as they have been prepared and cooled.

450 g/1 lb fresh thin egg noodles
2 tsp sesame oil
For the dressing:
4 tbsp sesame sauce
4 tbsp caster sugar
4 tbsp vinegar
4 tbsp Japanese soy sauce
4 tbsp chicken stock *(see page 25)*
1 cm/½ in fresh ginger
For the topping:
4 tsp dried *wakame* seaweed,
  soaked in hot water, then
  drained
200 g/7 oz tuna (in brine)
8 tbsp tinned sweetcorn
8 tbsp cooked prawns
1 punnet cress, rinsed

● Bring a large pan of water to the boil. Cook the noodles for 3 minutes, then rinse and drain. Toss in the sesame oil and place the noodles on to four serving plates.
● Mix the sesame sauce, sugar, vinegar, soy sauce and chicken stock well. Squeeze the juice from the ginger by grating the ginger first and then squeezing the juice from the ginger by hand. Add the squeezed juice from the ginger and mix again. Chill in the fridge.
● Divide the seaweed, tuna, sweetcorn, prawns and cress among each serving of the noodles.
● Pour the sesame dressing over and serve immediately.

chilled egg noodles with chicken and pepperoni

Pepperoni is not an authentic topping, but it really goes well with chilled noodles and gives an extra punch to this dish.

450 g/1 lb fresh or 300 g/11 oz
  dried thin egg noodles
1 tbsp sesame oil
For the sauce:
250 ml/9 fl oz chicken stock
  (see page 25)
120 ml/4 fl oz light soy sauce
4 tbsp caster sugar
120 ml/4 fl oz vinegar
4 tsp sesame oil
2 tbsp squeezed ginger juice
For the topping:
2 boneless chicken breasts
2 eggs, beaten
2 tsp caster sugar
1 tbsp vegetable oil
12 cm/5 in cucumber, thinly
  sliced diagonally and cut into
  long matchsticks
8 slices pepperoni, cut into long
  matchsticks
4 tsp red pickled ginger (*beni-
  shouga*) (optional)
4 tsp toasted sesame seeds

● Boil plenty of water in a pan and add the noodles. Cook for 3 minutes and rinse under the tap. Drain, then toss in the sesame oil. Put into four shallow dishes.
● To prepare the sauce, heat the stock, soy sauce and sugar in a pan and simmer for 3 minutes. Turn off the heat and add the vinegar, 4 tsp sesame oil and ginger juice. Mix well before chilling in the fridge.
● Boil the chicken in a pan for about 15–20 minutes. Let it cool and pull into shreds with your fingers or a knife. Set aside. Keep the water in the pan as stock for another use.
● Mix the beaten egg and sugar together in a bowl. Heat 1 teaspoon of oil in an omelette pan and pour a third of the egg mixture into it. When the egg is half set, turn it over. Repeat this to make two more thin omelettes, using fresh oil each time. When the omelettes are cooled, cut them in half and shred.
● Arrange the chicken, egg, cucumber and pepperoni on the noodles. Put the red pickled ginger (if using) on top and sprinkle with the sesame seeds. Pour the chilled sauce over prior to eating.

toasted sesame seeds

This is ever so easy to do. Just roast the sesame seeds in a frying pan without any oil. When the sesame seeds puff up and you can smell their aromatic flavour, they are ready. It is a good idea to roast a large amount of seeds and keep them in a jar for future use.

Right

Chilled Egg Noodles with Tuna, Prawn, Wakame and Sesame Sauce

chilled egg noodles with mackerel and prawn

Just perfect for one of those summer's days when you are hungry but can't face the thought of eating anything hot.

450 g/1 lb fresh or 300 g/11 oz dried thin egg noodles
For the sauce:
250 ml/9 fl oz chicken stock (see page 25)
120 ml/4 fl oz light soy sauce
4 tbsp caster sugar
120 ml/4 fl oz vinegar
4 tsp sesame oil
2 tbsp juice of squeezed ginger
For the topping:
100 g/4 oz bean sprouts
85 g/3½ oz mangetout
1 large fillet smoked mackerel, flaked
100 g/4 oz cooked prawns
½ punnet cress
1 medium-sized tomato, sliced

● Boil plenty of water in a pan, add the noodles and cook for 3 minutes. Rinse under water, drain and put into four shallow dishes.

● Heat the chicken stock, soy sauce and sugar in a pan and simmer for 3 minutes. Add the vinegar, sesame oil and ginger juice and mix well. Chill in the fridge.

● Blanch the bean sprouts and mangetout for 1 minute in boiling water. Remove and cut the mangetout into long matchsticks. Now arrange the mackerel flakes, prawns, bean sprouts, mangetout, cress and tomato on the noodles. Pour the chilled sauce over and serve at once.

chilled egg noodles with chicken and peanut sauce

A well-loved Chinese noodle dish. It can be prepared with any type of peanut butter, depending on your preference for smooth or crunchy.

450 g/1 lb boneless chicken breasts
450 g/1 lb fresh thin egg noodles
2 tsp sesame oil
25 cm/10 in cucumber, thinly sliced diagonally, then cut into long matchsticks
For the peanut sauce:
8 tbsp peanut butter
6 tbsp caster sugar
4 tbsp vinegar
5 tbsp chicken stock (see page 25)
3 tbsp light soy sauce
1 tbsp dark soy sauce
4 tsp sesame oil
3–4 tsp chilli oil

● Put the chicken in a large pan of water. Bring to the boil and simmer for 20 minutes, skimming off the scum from time to time. The poaching water can be put towards making stock. When the chicken is cooled, shred with your fingers or with a knife.

● Mix the peanut butter, sugar, vinegar, chicken stock, soy sauce, sesame oil and chilli oil together in a bowl.

● Bring a large pan of water to the boil and add the noodles. Cook for 3 minutes, rinse and drain. Toss in the sesame oil. Put the noodles on to the individual plates.

● Place a quarter of the shredded chicken and cucumber on to each serving of noodles. Pour the sesame sauce over and serve immediately.

Right

Chilled Egg Noodles with Chicken and Peanut Sauce

chilled udon with five toppings

Dried medium-sized *udon* is preferable for this dish if you can obtain them. A non-stick omelette pan will help you to prepare the egg sheets which should resemble thin pancakes.

400 g/14 oz dried or 600 g/1¼ lb
  parboiled fresh udon
500 ml/18 fl oz dipping broth
  (see page 26), **chilled**
For the toppings:
2 eggs
2 tsp caster sugar
1 tbsp vegetable oil
8 okra
salt
4 tsp dried *wakame* seaweed,
  soaked in warm water and
  drained
8 seafood sticks, torn into
  shreds
½ punnet cress

● Boil plenty of water in a pan. Add the *udon* and cook 8–15 minutes for dried or 3 minutes for fresh *udon*. Rinse and put the *udon* into four shallow bowls.

● Mix the eggs and sugar together in a bowl. Heat the oil in a frying pan and pour in a third of the egg mixture. When the egg starts bubbling, turn it over. (The method is the same as for making thin pancakes.) Repeat this and make two more egg sheets. Let them cool and then cut in half and cut into shreds.

● Sprinkle the salt over the okra on a chopping board, then roll the okra with salt to remove the fine down. Boil some water in a pan and blanch the okra for just a minute before chopping finely.

● Arrange the shredded egg, okra, *wakame*, seafood shreds and cress in separate groups on top of the *udon*.

● Just before eating, pour over the chilled dipping broth.

chilled udon with fermented soya beans

Fermented soya beans, or *natto*, are not to everyone's taste. Even in Japan, where it originated, *natto* is very much a "love it or hate it" food despite it being a nutritious source of protein. Give it a try. You never know – you might like it! *Natto* is available from Japanese food stores.

400 g/14 oz dried or 600 g/1¼ lb
  parboiled fresh udon
500 ml/18 fl oz dipping broth
  (see page 26), **chilled**
For the topping:
6 okra
salt
200 g/7 oz Japanese fermented
  soya beans (natto)
5 g/¼ oz bonito flakes (katsuo
  bushi)
1 spring onion, chopped
1 tsp hot prepared mustard
4 tsp Japanese soy sauce
½ sheet *nori*, shredded

● Remove the tiny hairs on the okra, the easiest way to do this is to first sprinkle the salt over the okra and roll over on a chopping board. Blanch in the boiling water for 1 minute, drain and chop.

● Mix the okra, *natto*, bonito flakes, spring onion, mustard and soy sauce together in a bowl.

● Bring plenty of water to the boil in a large pan and add the *udon*. Cook according to the instructions on the packet. Rinse and drain. Divide the *udon* into four bowls.

● Pile the *natto* mixture on top of the udon. Gently pour the dipping broth over and sprinkle with *nori*, then serve immediately.

Right

*Chilled
Udon with
Fermented
Soya Beans*

chilled udon with aubergine and miso sauce

Miso sauce is a versatile performer that can be paired with almost any vegetable you care to mention. Here it is combined with aubergine which should be soaked in salted water to remove any trace of bitterness.

500 ml/18 fl oz *dashi* broth
  (see page 26)
4 tbsp vinegar
400 g/14 oz dried or 600 g/1¼ lb
  parboiled fresh *udon*
For the topping:
1 tbsp sunflower oil
2 cloves garlic, minced
1 cm/½ in fresh ginger, peeled
  and minced
8 spring onions, chopped
200 g/7 oz aubergine, cut into
  matchstick-sized pieces and
  soaked in salted water
200 g/7 oz small green pepper,
  cut into matchstick-sized
  pieces
a pinch of salt
4 tbsp *miso* paste
1 tbsp Japanese soy sauce
2 tsp caster sugar
3 tbsp Japanese rice wine (*sake*)

● Mix the *dashi* broth and vinegar and chill in the fridge. Heat the oil in a frying pan. Add the garlic, ginger and spring onion and fry for one minute.

● Add the aubergine, green pepper and salt and stir fry for 4–5 minutes or until the aubergine is softened. Add the *miso* paste, soy sauce, sugar and *sake* and stir well. Set aside.

● Boil plenty of water in a pan and add the *udon*. Cook for 4–5 minutes for fresh or 8–15 minutes for dried *udon* or according to the instruction on the packet. Rinse with cold water. Drain and divide into four bowls.

● Place the aubergine mixture on the *udon* and pour the broth over. Serve immediately.

Right
Chilled Udon with Aubergine and Miso Sauce

chilled soba with nameko mushrooms

A light, refreshing lunch or part of a dinner that is quickly prepared and easily digested.

400 g/14 oz dried *soba*
approx 400 g/14 oz tinned
   ***nameko* mushrooms**
300 g/11 oz *mooli* or *daikon*,
   peeled and grated
½ sheet nori seaweed, shredded
500 ml/18 fl oz dipping broth
   (see page 26), chilled

● Boil plenty of water in a large pan and add the *soba*. Cook for 5–6 minutes or according to the instruction on the packet. Rinse under the tap and drain well. Put the *soba* into four bowls.
● Mix the mushrooms and *mooli* or *daikon* together in a bowl. Pile them on to the *soba* and sprinkle with the *nori*. Gently pour the chilled dipping broth over just before serving.

chilled soba with bean curd sheet

A refreshing summertime treat. There is nothing quite like chilled *soba* and a good dipping broth to restore heat-jaded appetites.

400 g/14 oz dried *soba*
500 ml/18 fl oz dipping broth
   (see page 26), chilled
For the topping:
2 bean curd sheet (*abura-age*)
1 tbsp vegetable oil
8 *shiitake* mushrooms, sliced
salt and pepper
2 tsp soy sauce
1 punnet cress, rinsed
3 spring onions, chopped

● Pierce two sides of the *abura-age* with skewers and grill directly over a gas ring or grill for about 50 seconds on each side. Slice into thin strips and set aside.
● Heat the oil in a pan and fry the mushrooms for about 2 minutes. Season with salt and pepper and sprinkle with the soy sauce. Set aside.
● Bring plenty of water to the boil in a large saucepan. Add the *soba* and cook for 5–6 minutes. Drain and rinse well under cold running water. Drain again and divide into four portions.
● Mix the *abura-age*, mushrooms and cress together well in a bowl. Divide among the four servings and sprinkle with spring onion. Pour the dipping broth over just before serving.

chilled soba with sour plum sauce

The bite of the sour plums in the dipping broth gives an extra zest to this cold noodle dish.

4 spring onions, sliced
3 boneless chicken breasts
12 okra
salt
400 g/14 oz dried *soba*
For the soured plum sauce:
4 large sour plums (*umeboshi*),
   seeded and chopped finely
500 ml/18 fl oz dipping broth
   (see page 26)

● Soak the sliced spring onions in cold water until ready for use. Cook the chicken in boiling water for about 15 minutes or until cooked. When cooled, pull the meat into small strips using your fingers.
● Sprinkle the okra with salt and roll each on a chopping board to remove the hairs. Cook for around a minute in boiling water, then cut into 1 cm/½ in slices.
● Put the soured plums into a mortar. Add a little broth and grind roughly into a thin paste. Return the mixture to the dipping broth and chill in the fridge.
● Bring plenty of water to the boil in a large saucepan. Add the *soba* and cook for 5–6 minutes. Drain and rinse well under cold running water. Drain again. Mix the *soba* with the spring onions in a bowl and then divide into four portions.
● Add the chicken and okra. Pour the soured plum dipping broth over and serve at once.

Left
*Chilled
Soba with
Nameko
Mushrooms*

chilled soba with deep-fried mackerel

Mackerel is one of the great mainstays of the Japanese diet. It is not only eaten raw as sushi and sashimi but incorporated in many Japanese cooked dishes, as here.

400 g/14 oz dried *soba*
500 ml/18 fl oz dipping broth
  (see page 26)
For the topping:
vegetable oil for deep frying
8 tbsp plain flour
120 ml/4 fl oz water
450 g/1 lb mackerel, gutted and
  filleted and cut into four
  pieces per person
350 g/12 oz *mooli* or *daikon*,
  peeled and grated
2 spring onions, chopped
½ punnet cress

● Heat the cooking oil in a saucepan to 180°C/350°F. Mix the flour and water lightly in a bowl to a lumpy consistency to make a batter, then dip the mackerel pieces in. Deep fry for about 3 minutes or until golden brown.
● Bring plenty of water to the boil in a large saucepan. Add the *soba* and cook for 5–6 minutes. Drain and rinse well under cold running water. Drain again and then divide into four portions.
● Place four pieces of deep-fried mackerel in each bowl. Place the grated *mooli* or *daikon* in the centre and garnish with the spring onions and cress. Pour the dipping broth over and serve immediately.

chilled soba with shredded daikon

Japanese *daikon* is the ideal ingredient for this dish but is quite hard to come by unless there happens to be a Japanese food store nearby. I find that *mooli* makes an acceptable stand-in.

400 g/14 oz dried *soba*
300 g/11 oz *daikon* or *mooli*,
  peeled and shredded
½ punnet cress, rinsed
1 sheet nori seaweed, shredded
750 ml/1¼ pt dipping broth
  (see page 26)
For the garnishes:
2 spring onions, chopped
2.5 cm/1 in fresh ginger, grated
2 *myoga* (optional), shredded

● Bring plenty of water to the boil in a large saucepan. Add the soba and cook for 5–6 minutes. Rinse and cool in cold water. Drain.
● Mix the *soba, daikon* and cress well in a bowl. Divide into individual serving bowls and sprinkle with the *nori*. Serve with the chilled dipping broth and garnishes on a separate small dish.

Right
Chilled Soba with Shredded Daikon

classic cold somen

A cool, refreshing and easily digested dish for those hot summer days when you can't face eating anything hot or heavy.

400–500 g/14 oz–1 lb 2 oz *somen*
750 ml/1¼ pt chilled dipping broth (see page 26)
For the garnish:
1 sheet *nori*, shredded
3 spring onions, chopped
2 tsp *wasabi* mustard
8 leaves Bowles' mint (*oba*), shredded
ice cubes

● Put the *somen* noodles into a pan of boiling water. When the water returns to the boil, add 100 ml/¼ pt water to reduce the temperature again. The second time the water comes back to the boil, the *somen* will be ready. Drain well and rinse with cold water. Drain again.

● Place the ice cubes on a communal plate and put all the *somen* on top of the ice to keep it cool. Each diner takes *somen* as required using chopsticks. Serve the dipping broth cold in small cups or boats, with the garnish also served on small, individual dishes.

How to eat *somen*

Place some of the garnish in to your dipping broth, then take some of the *somen* from the communal plate with your chopsticks, dip into the broth, then slurp up with your lips.

Left *Classic Cold Somen*

chilled soba with vegetable tempura

Tempura or deep-fried vegetables are one of the most famous Japanese dishes. Both the tempura and *soba* should be dipped into the broth as you eat.

vegetable oil for deep frying
For the batter:
1 egg, beaten
9 tbsp plain flour
240 ml/8½ fl oz cold water
170 g/6 oz aubergine, halved and sliced
4 *shiitake* mushrooms
110 g/4 oz carrots, cut into long matchsticks
16 green beans
400 g/14 oz dried *soba*
750 ml/1¼ pt dipping broth (see page 26), chilled

● Fill a saucepan ⅓ full with the oil and heat to 180°C/350°F. Mix the egg, flour and water lightly in a bowl. Dip the aubergine and *shiitake* mushrooms in the batter and deep fry until golden. Dip the carrots and green beans in the batter in small bundles and deep fry. Drain on absorbent paper.

● Boil plenty of water in a pan, add the *soba* and cook for 4–6 minutes or according to the instructions on the packet. Rinse and drain well.

● Put the *soba* on four plates and divide the *tempura* onto four separate plates. Fill four small cups with the dipping broth. Serve at once.

chilled somen with sesame dipping

Fried vegetables make the chilled *somen* more nutritious and filling, while the combination of the sesame sauce and dipping broth impart a rich and delicate flavour. It is a good idea to make the dipping broth in advance; it will keep in the fridge for a few days.

400 g/14 oz somen
For the sesame dipping broth:
500 ml/18 fl oz dipping broth
 (see page 26)
1 cm/½ in fresh ginger, peeled, grated and squeezed by hand for the juice
5 tbsp sesame sauce
2 spring onions, finely chopped
For the topping:
sunflower oil for frying
300 g/11 oz aubergine, thinly sliced and soaked in salted water
4 large shiitake mushrooms
1 small green pepper
4 myoga (optional), finely chopped

● Heat the dipping broth and add the ginger juice and sesame sauce. When it comes to the boil, add the spring onions and turn off the heat. Chill in the fridge.

● Bring plenty of water to the boil in a pan and add the *somen*. When the water returns to boil, add half a cupful of cold water. The second time the water comes back to the boil, the *somen* will be ready. Rinse with the cold water and drain. Put the *somen* on to four plates.

● Heat 2 tablespoons of oil in a frying pan. Fry the aubergine first, then the mushrooms and pepper. If you need more oil, add another 2 tablespoons.

● Place the aubergine, mushrooms and pepper beside the *somen* and, if using, put the sliced *myoga* on top. Serve immediately with small bowls of dipping broth.

chilled somen with pork

An invigorating combination of chilled noodles with pork and broccoli stir-fried in a hot *toban* sauce.

400 g/14 oz somen
500 ml/18 fl oz dipping broth
 (see page 26), **chilled**
For the topping:
1½ tbsp vegetable oil
4 cloves garlic, sliced
360 g/12 oz lean pork, sliced on a slant into bite-sized pieces
1 tbsp mirin
2½ tbsp soy sauce
2 tsp chilli bean sauce (toban djan)
8 small broccoli florets
a pinch of salt

● Heat the oil in a pan, then add the garlic and fry for about a minute. Add the meat and fry for a further 2–3 minutes. Then add the mirin, soy sauce and chilli bean sauce and stir fry for 2 minutes.

● Bring plenty of water to the boil in a large saucepan. Add the *somen* and cook for 1–2 minutes. Drain and rinse well under cold running water. Drain again and then divide into four portions.

● Meanwhile, bring a pan of water to the boil, add a pinch of salt and boil the broccoli for 1–2 minutes. Drain and rinse.

● Place the meat and broccoli in to the four bowls. Serve immediately after pouring in the chilled dipping broth.

Right
Chilled Somen with Pork

[76]

bean thread noodle salad with barbecued pork

The secret of success with this dish is to have good quality pork well marinated in *cha siu* sauce and roasted long enough to be edible but not so long as to overcook the centre of the meat, which should remain slightly rare.

200 g/7 oz bean thread noodles
100 g/4 oz carrots, cut into
  matchsticks
200 g/7 oz cucumber, cut into
  matchsticks
200 g/7 oz Chinese barbecued
  pork (*cha siu*) (see page 34),
  shredded
2 dried black ear fungi, soaked
  and shredded or 2–3 shiitake
  mushrooms
4 tsp toasted sesame seeds
  (see page 63)
For the dressing:
4 tbsp light soy sauce
2½ tbsp dark soy sauce
2½ tbsp caster sugar
5 tbsp vinegar
4 tbsp sesame oil

● Soak the bean thread noodles in warm water for 5 minutes or according to the instructions on the packet. Rinse under water and drain.

● Mix the soy sauce, sugar, vinegar and sesame oil together in a bowl. Add the carrots, cucumber, *cha siu* pork, black ear fungus and noodles and mix well.

● Serve the noodles either on a large dish or in four individual dishes and sprinkle with toasted sesame seeds before eating.

bean thread noodle salad with prawns

yam woonsen

Yam woonsen is a hot Thai salad. *Nam pla*, an essential ingredient used in Thai cuisine, enhances the flavour of the dish. It is a good idea to prepare this salad at least 30 minutes before you serve it to allow the full sweet, hot flavour to mature.

200 g/7 oz bean thread noodles
16 tiger prawns, peeled and
  deveined
1 tsp fish sauce (*nam pla*)
2 tsp freshly squeezed lemon
  juice
1 tsp palm or brown sugar
1 tbsp sunflower oil
1 small red pepper, finely
  chopped
2 sticks celery, thinly sliced
110 g/4 oz carrots, cut into
  matchsticks
2 spring onions, chopped
4–5 lettuce leaves
coriander leaves
For the dressing:
2 shallots, finely chopped
1 dry red chilli, crushed
3 small green chilli, chopped
4 tbsp fish sauce (*nam pla*)
120 ml/4 fl oz freshly squeezed
  lemon juice (about 2 lemons)
4½ tbsp palm or brown sugar
1 tbsp sunflower oil

● Soak the bean thread noodles in warm water for 5 minutes or according to the instructions on the packet. Rinse under cold running water and drain.

● Marinate the prawns in 1 tsp of fish sauce, 2 tsp of lemon juice and 1 tsp of sugar for 15 minutes.

● Meanwhile, mix together the dressing ingredients.

● Heat 1 tbsp of oil in a frying pan and stir fry the prawns thoroughly.

● Put the red pepper, celery, carrot, spring onion and noodles in a bowl and mix together. Place 1 lettuce leaf on each plate and pile the noodle mixture on it. Put the prawns on the noodles and sprinkle over the coriander leaves.

Right

Bean
Thread
Noodle
Salad with
Prawns

stir-fried noodles

Chow mein must be the most famous stir-fried noodle dish in the west. This quick method using a wok creates mouthwatering noodle dishes in minutes. Stir-fried egg noodles, rice noodles, or udon are widely eaten in south-east Asia, each country adding its own particular flavouring.

stir-fried egg noodles with barbecued pork

Literally translated as "stir-fried noodles", *chow mein* is an archetypal noodle fast food and one of the first noodle dishes to become popularized in the West.

**450 g/1 lb fresh or 280 g/10 oz
   dried thin egg noodles**
2 tbsp vegetable oil
**2.5 cm/1 in fresh ginger, peeled
   and minced**
2 cloves garlic, minced
1 medium onion, sliced
**150 g/6 oz carrots, sliced into
   bite-sized pieces**
12 mangetout, blanched
225 g/8 oz bean sprouts, rinsed
**225 g/8 oz Chinese barbecued
   pork (cha siu) (see page 34),
   sliced and cut into bite-sized
   squares**
1 tbsp sesame oil
4 tbsp light soy sauce
1 tbsp dark soy sauce
1 tbsp caster sugar
salt and black pepper

● Boil plenty of water in a pan and cook the noodles for 3 minutes. Rinse under the tap and drain.

● Heat the vegetable oil in a wok or frying pan until very hot. Stir fry the ginger and garlic for 30 seconds. Add the onion, carrots and mangetout and stir fry for 2 minutes. Add the bean sprouts and *cha siu* pork and stir-fry for another 2 minutes.

● Add the sesame oil, noodles, soy sauce and sugar and stir fry for 1 minute until the noodles are coated with sauce. Season if necessary and stir once more. Serve immediately.

stir-fried egg noodles with yakisoba sauce

Maybe the most popular noodle dish eaten in Japan and found in noodle shops, at home and made and served in the street at festivals or cooked over a camp fire for lunch during a trip out into the countryside. If *yakisoba* sauce is unavailable make your own (see page 88).

**310 g/11 oz dried egg noodles
   or 600 g/1¼ lb Japanese
   steamed noodles**
1 tbsp sesame oil
2 tbsp sunflower oil
**225 g/8 oz boneless belly of
   pork or chicken breasts,
   thinly sliced**
1 medium-sized onion, sliced
**100 g/4 oz carrots, cut in half
   lengthwise and thinly sliced**
5 cabbage leaves, roughly cut
salt and black pepper
**7 tbsp *yakisoba* or Japanese
   brown sauce**
***nori* flakes (*ao-nori*) (optional)**
**red pickled ginger (*beni-shouga*)
   (optional)**

● If using dried noodles, boil plenty of water in a pan, add the noodles and cook for 3 minutes. Rinse with water and drain. Toss in the sesame oil. If you use Japanese steamed noodles, just rinse with very hot water.

● Heat the sunflower oil in a wok or frying pan, then fry the pork for 3–4 minutes. Add the onions, carrots and cabbage and stir fry for 3–4 minutes. Sprinkle with the salt and pepper, add the noodles and *yakisoba* or brown sauce and stir well.

● Put the noodles on to four plates and sprinkle with the *nori* flakes and pickled ginger. Serve at once.

Right
*Stir-fried
Egg
Noodles
with
Yakisoba
Sauce*

stir-fried egg noodles with vegetables

chow mein with vegetables

450 g/I lb fresh or 280 g/10 oz
    dried medium egg noodles
2 tbsp vegetable oil
2.5 cm/I in fresh ginger, peeled
    and minced
2 cloves garlic, minced
280 g/10 oz Chinese cabbage,
    chopped into bite-sized
    squares
200 g/7 oz bean sprouts
I small red pepper, cut into
    bite-sized squares
I small green pepper, cut into
    bite-sized squares
16 straw mushrooms (tinned),
    halved
I tbsp sesame oil
2 spring onions, chopped
4 tbsp light soy sauce
I tbsp dark soy sauce
I tbsp caster sugar
salt and black pepper

● Boil plenty of water in a pan and cook the noodles for 3–4 minutes. Rinse under cold water and drain.

● Heat the vegetable oil in a wok or frying pan, then stir fry the ginger and garlic for 30 seconds. Add the Chinese cabbage, bean sprouts, red and green peppers and straw mushrooms. Stir each ingredient as you add it. Fry together for about 2 minutes.

● Add the sesame oil, noodles, spring onions, soy sauce and sugar and stir well. Check the taste, adding salt and pepper if necessary. Put the noodles on to four plates and serve at once.

Right

*Stir-fried
Egg
Noodles
with
Vegetables*

stir-fried egg noodles with prawns and black bean sauce

These stir-fried noodles require cooking for only a short time. Tiger prawns add both flavour and a certain luxury to this dish, so if you are feeling extravagant, use them in place of their smaller cousins.

450 g/1 lb fresh or 280 g/10 oz dried medium egg noodles

3 tbsp vegetable oil

2.5 cm/1 in fresh ginger, peeled and minced

3 cloves garlic, minced

100 g/4 oz peeled prawns

12 tiger or large prawns, peeled and deveined

1 small red pepper, sliced

4 spring onions, chopped into 2.5 cm/1 in lengths

black pepper

1 tbsp sesame oil

4 tsp light soy sauce

4 tsp dark soy sauce

2 tbsp Chinese rice wine or dry sherry

3 tbsp black bean sauce

● Cook the noodles in a pan of boiling water for 4 minutes. Rinse and drain well.

● Heat the vegetable oil in a wok or frying pan. Stir fry the ginger and garlic for 30 seconds. Add the prawns, red pepper, spring onion and a sprinkling of black pepper and stir for 1–2 minutes or until the prawns are heated thoroughly.

● Add the sesame oil and noodles and stir. Add the soy sauce, rice wine and black bean sauce, then stir again until the noodles are coated well with the sauce.

● Put the noodles on to four plates and serve at once.

Malaysian spicy egg noodles

This dish uses *belacan*, the pungent shrimp based paste commonly used in Malaysian and Thai cooking. Don't let the odour put you off when you use *belacan* but be warned that the aroma does tend to stick around unless you ensure your kitchen is well ventilated while you are cooking!

280 g/10 oz dried medium egg noodles

5 tbsp vegetable oil

4–6 small dried red chillies, soaked in hot water, then ground

2 cloves garlic, finely chopped

1 tsp dried shrimp paste (*belacan*) (optional)

280 g/10 oz rump steak, thinly sliced

1 medium-sized onion, thinly sliced

2 green chillies, chopped

200 g/7 oz bean sprouts

100 g/4 oz mustard greens or fresh spinach

salt and black pepper

3 tbsp light soy sauce

coriander leaves

4 lime wedges

● Boil plenty of water in a pan and cook the noodles for 4 minutes. Rinse under water and drain. Set aside.

● Heat 3 tablespoons of the oil in a wok or frying pan. Add the chillies, garlic and *belacan* and stir. Add the beef and fry for 2–3 minutes.

● Add the onion, green chillies, bean sprouts and mustard greens, stirring each time you add the ingredients. Season with salt and pepper.

● Add the remaining oil and the egg noodles, sprinkle soy sauce over the mixture and mix all the ingredients well. Put the noodles on to 4 plates and garnish with coriander leaves and lime wedges. Serve at once.

Right

Malaysian
Spicy Egg
Noodles

Indonesian fried egg noodles with chicken and bean curd

mie goreng

Indonesian cooking has become increasingly popular over the last few years and mie goreng, one of the most commonly eaten dishes in Indonesia, has been at the forefront of this trend.

280 g/10 oz dried medium egg
 noodles
4 tbsp + 2 tsp vegetable oil
280 g/10 oz bean curd (*tofu*),
 diced
2 eggs, beaten
2.5 cm/1 in fresh ginger, peeled
 and minced
4 shallots, finely chopped
1 tsp ground coriander
1 red chilli, chopped
225 g/8 oz boneless chicken
 breasts, diced
100 g/4 oz carrots, sliced
3 sticks celery, sliced
4 spring onions, chopped into
 2.5 cm/1 in lengths
3 tbsp light soy sauce
salt and pepper
4 tomato wedges
sliced cucumber

● Cook the egg noodles in a pan of boiling water for 4 minutes. Rinse and drain well.

● Heat 1 tablespoon of the oil in a wok or frying pan and fry the bean curd until lightly browned. Set aside and clean the wok.

● To make the egg sheets, heat 1 teaspoon of the oil in an omelette pan. Add half the beaten egg and fry both

sides, like a thin pancake. Repeat to make a second egg sheet. When the egg sheets are cooled, slice them thinly.

● Heat another 2 tablespoons of the oil in the wok, stir fry the ginger, shallots, ground coriander and red chilli for 30 seconds. Add the chicken and stir for 2–3 minutes. Add the carrots, celery, bean curd and spring onion, stirring each time you add the ingredients.

● Add the final tablespoon of oil, the noodles and soy sauce to the wok. Season with salt and pepper if required, and stir well. Divide the noodles on to four plates, sprinkle the sliced egg sheets on top and garnish with tomato wedges and cucumber slices. Serve at once.

stir-fried udon with yakisoba sauce

English brown sauce has a stronger, sourer flavour than Japanese brown sauce. If you cannot obtain *yakisoba* sauce or Japanese brown sauce, try making your own (see below).

600 g/1 lb 5 oz parboiled fresh
 or 400 g/14 oz dried *udon*
3 tbsp sunflower oil
225 g/8 oz minced pork
1 medium-sized onion, sliced
250 g/9 oz Chinese cabbage,
 sliced
½ red pepper, sliced
150 g/6 oz mangetout, cut in
 half
salt and black pepper

8 tbsp *yakisoba* or Japanese
 brown sauce
***nori* flakes (*ao-nori*) (optional)**
red pickled ginger (*beni-shouga*)
 (optional)

● Rinse the parboiled *udon* with very hot water or, if using dried *udon*, cook according to the instructions on the packet.

● Heat the oil in a wok or frying pan until very hot. Add the pork and fry for 3 minutes. Add the onion, Chinese cabbage, red pepper and mangetout and stir fry for about 3 minutes. Season with salt and pepper.

● Add the *udon* and *yakisoba* or Japanese brown sauce and stir well. Divide the *udon* on to four plates. Sprinkle *nori* flakes and pickled ginger over and serve immediately.

yakisoba sauce

5–6 servings

5 tbsp brown sauce
4 tbsp light soy sauce
4 tsp tomato ketchup
4 tsp oyster sauce
4 tbsp caster sugar

Mix all the ingredients together

stir-fried udon with seafood

Stir frying coaxes maximum flavour out of the seafood ingredients and gives the *udon* noodles a smooth, slippery texture in this filling dish.

400 g/14 oz dried or 600 g/1¼ lb parboiled fresh *udon*
3 tbsp sunflower oil
150 g/6 oz squid, cleaned and sliced
150 g/6 oz peeled prawns
4 spring onions, chopped roughly
225 g/8 oz bean sprouts
280 g/10 oz *shimeji* mushrooms, roots cut off and separated, or 15 *shiitake* mushrooms, sliced
4 tsp dried *wakame* seaweed, soaked in hot water
4 tbsp bonito flakes (*katsuobushi*)
4 tbsp Japanese soy sauce
salt and black pepper

● Boil plenty of water in a large pan and add the *udon*. Cook for 7–15 minutes for dried, or 3 minutes for parboiled fresh *udon*. Rinse under the tap and drain.

● Heat the oil in a wok or frying pan until very hot. Stir fry the squid and prawns for 2 minutes. Add the spring onions, bean sprouts, mushrooms and *wakame* and stir fry for about 2 minutes.

● Add the *udon*, bonito flakes and soy sauce and stir. Season with salt and pepper. Stir for another minute and serve at once.

stir-fried udon with curry sauce

This is a rather *nouveau* way of cooking *udon* in Japan. However, hot *udon* soup with curry sauce is very popular, which must prove that curry and *udon* make a good combination.

600 g/1¼ lb parboiled fresh or 400 g/14 oz dried *udon*
4 tbsp sunflower oil
1 large clove garlic, minced
1 medium-sized onion, sliced
1 small red pepper, sliced
300 g/11 oz aubergine, quartered lengthwise and sliced into 1 cm/½ in wedges
150 g/6 oz button mushrooms, sliced
For the sauce:
2 tbsp hot water
½ vegetable or chicken stock cube, crumbled
4 tbsp tomato ketchup
1–2 tsp hot curry powder
½ tsp salt
coriander leaves to garnish

● Boil plenty of water in a large pan and add the *udon*. Cook dried *udon* according to the instructions on the packet, and fresh *udon* for 3 minutes. Rinse under cold water and drain.

● Heat the oil in a wok or frying pan until very hot. Add the garlic and onion and stir fry for 1 minute. Then add the red pepper, aubergines and mushrooms and stir fry for about 4–5 minutes or until the aubergines have softened.

● Mix the hot water, stock cube, tomato ketchup, curry powder and salt together in a bowl to make a curry sauce. Add the *udon* and curry mixture to the vegetables and stir fry for a further 1–2 minutes. Garnish with the coriander leaves and serve immediately.

Right
Stir-fried Udon with Curry Sauce

stir-fried rice vermicelli with liver and chives

Rice vermicelli is light and easy to digest. This Chinese dish is usually served as a light lunch dish. As the liver is marinated in rice wine and soy sauce, the taste of the liver, which some people tend to find offputting, is reduced. You can use any liver, though this recipe uses chicken.

225 g/8 oz rice vermicelli
450 g/1 lb chicken liver, sliced
2 tsp light soy sauce
1 tsp Chinese rice wine or dry
 sherry
1 tbsp cornflour
3 tbsp vegetable oil
2 cloves garlic, minced
2.5 cm/1 in fresh ginger, peeled
 and minced
225 g/8 oz bean sprouts
8 dried *shiitake* mushrooms,
 soaked in hot water, then
 sliced
225 g/8 oz Chinese green chives
 or spring onion, cut into 5 cm/
 2 in lengths
salt
For the sauce:
1 tbsp sesame oil
4 tbsp chicken stock *(see page 25)*
1 tbsp Chinese rice wine or dry
 sherry
2½ tbsp light soy sauce
4 tsp dark soy sauce
2 tsp oyster sauce
1 tsp caster sugar
black pepper

● Soak the vermicelli in warm water for 3 minutes or according to the instructions on the packet. Rinse under cold water and drain. Blanch the liver in boiling water until it turns white. Then marinate the liver in the soy sauce, rice wine and cornflour for about 20 minutes.

● Heat 2 tbsp of the oil in a wok or frying pan. Stir fry the liver for 3–4 minutes before adding the garlic and ginger. Stir well. Add the remaining tablespoon of oil, bean sprouts, mushrooms and green chives or spring onions and stir fry for 1–2 minutes.

● Add sauce ingredients and the vermicelli and stir until the sauce is all absorbed. Taste and season with the salt if required. Divide the noodles on to four plates and serve at once.

stir-fried udon with miso sauce

This is another *nouveau* stir-fried *udon* dish. The *udon* are coated in a salty sauce, making a very appetising fast food.

400 g/14 oz dried or 600 g/1¼ lb
 parboiled fresh *udon*
200 g/7 oz green cabbage
125 g/5 oz fresh green beans
3 tbsp sunflower oil
225 g/8 oz rump steak, sliced on
 a slant into bite-sized pieces
1 small red pepper, chopped
 into bite-sized pieces
10 *shiitake* mushrooms,
 quartered
a pinch of salt and chilli powder
2 tbsp red *miso* paste
2 tbsp Japanese soy sauce
2 tbsp mirin
1 spring onion, chopped

● Boil plenty of water in a large pan and cook dried *udon* for 7–15 minutes or parboiled fresh *udon* for 3 minutes. Rinse under tap and drain.

● Blanch the cabbage leaves and green beans for 2 minutes. Rinse under cold water. Cut the cabbage leaves into bite-sized pieces and halve the green beans.

● Heat the oil in a wok or frying pan until very hot. Add the beef and fry for 2–3 minutes. Add the cabbage, green beans and *shiitake* mushrooms and sprinkle on salt and chilli powder. Stir fry for another 2–3 minutes.

● Mix the *miso*, soy sauce and mirin together in a bowl. Add the *udon* and *miso* mixture to the pan and stir fry for about a minute. Put the *udon* on to four plates. Sprinkle the chopped spring onion over and serve at once.

Right
Stir-fried
Udon with
Miso Sauce

Thai fried vermicelli with red curry paste

Thai red curry paste is a result of the influence of Indian and Chinese cooking. The result is a novel and interesting combination of heat and sourness.

225 g/8 oz rice vermicelli
3 tbsp vegetable oil
225 g/8 oz bean curd (*tofu*) diced
3 cloves garlic, chopped
100 g/4 oz tinned bamboo shoots
225 g/8 oz bean sprouts
100 g/4 oz mustard greens or fresh spinach
2 tbsp Thai red curry paste
6 tbsp fish sauce (*nam pla*)
3 tbsp light soy sauce
1 tbsp palm or brown sugar
coriander leaves
4 lime wedges

● Soak the rice vermicelli in warm water for 3–5 minutes. Rinse and drain.

● Heat the oil in a wok or frying pan and fry bean curd until golden brown. Add the garlic, bamboo shoots, bean sprouts and mustard greens or spinach, stirring each time you add the ingredients.

● Add the red curry paste, fish sauce, soy sauce and brown sugar, then stir well. Add the vermicelli and stir until the noodles are well coated with sauce.

● Put the vermicelli on to four plates and garnish with coriander leaves and lime wedges. Serve at once.

stir-fried rice vermicelli with barbecued pork and prawns

Another Chinese noodle dish using *cha siu* to provide extra flavour. If you do not have time to make *cha siu*, you can use sliced lean pork instead.

225 g/8 oz rice vermicelli
4 tbsp vegetable oil
2.5 cm/1 in fresh ginger, peeled and minced
2 cloves garlic, minced
225 g/8 oz Chinese barbecued pork (*cha siu*) (*see page 34*), diced
100 g/4 oz peeled prawns
200 g/7 oz bean sprouts
8 water chestnuts, sliced
6 spring onions, chopped
100 g/4 oz spinach, chopped
2 tbsp Chinese rice wine or dry sherry
4 tbsp light soy sauce
1½ tbsp dark soy sauce
6 tbsp chicken stock (*see page 25*)
black pepper and salt

● Soak the vermicelli in warm water for 3 minutes or according to the instructions on the packet. Rinse under the tap and drain.

● Heat 3 tablespoons of the oil in a wok or large frying pan until very hot. Stir fry the ginger and garlic for 30 seconds. Add the pork, prawns, bean sprouts, water chestnuts, spring onions and spinach and stir-fry for 2–3 minutes.

● Add the remaining tablespoon of oil and the vermicelli, stir quickly, then add the rice wine, soy sauce and chicken stock. Keep stirring until the sauce is absorbed. Sprinkle with black pepper and salt to taste. Serve immediately.

Right

Stir-fried Rice Vermicelli with Barbecued Pork and Prawns

Singapore spicy noodles

The return home of itinerant Chinese over the years has resulted in a gradual increase in the popularity of curried dishes in China, especially in the south-western provinces. Although the origins of this dish lie in India, Singapore has been the cultural melting pot where most Chinese migrants have come into contact with Indian cuisine.

225 g/8 oz rice vermicelli
4 tbsp vegetable oil
2 cloves garlic, minced
1 cm/½ in fresh ginger, peeled and minced
1 red chilli, chopped
100 g/4 oz peeled prawns
6 small squid, cleaned and sliced
225 g/8 oz bean sprouts
100 g/4 oz spinach
225 g/8 oz Chinese barbecued pork (*cha siu*) (*see page 34*), thinly sliced
2 eggs, beaten
3 spring onions, roughly chopped
⅔ tsp salt
a pinch of chilli powder
black pepper
2–3 tsp hot curry powder
1 tbsp light soy sauce
2 tsp caster sugar
150 ml/¼ pt chicken stock (*see page 25*)

● Soak the rice vermicelli in warm water for 3 minutes or according to the instructions on the packet. Rinse with cold water and drain.

● Heat 3 tablespoons of the oil in a wok or frying pan until very hot. Add the garlic, ginger and red chilli and stir fry for 30 seconds.

● Add the prawns and squid and stir for another minute. Then add the bean sprouts, spinach and pork and stir fry for 1–2 minutes.

● Make a well in the centre, add the beaten egg and scramble lightly. Quickly add the remaining tablespoon of oil and the rice vermicelli and mix all the ingredients well.

● Add the spring onion, salt, chilli powder, black pepper, curry powder, soy sauce, caster sugar and chicken stock. Stir until the sauce is all absorbed. Put the noodles on to four plates and serve at once.

Right
Singapore Spicy Noodles

Indonesian fried vermicelli with squid

Squid is a great favourite throughout Asia and nowhere more so than in Indonesia. The flavourings used here are distinct but without being so powerful as to cloak the taste of the seafood.

225 g/8 oz rice vermicelli
3 tbsp vegetable oil
2.5 cm/1 in fresh ginger, peeled and minced
4 shallots, chopped finely
8 small squid, cleaned and sliced
100 g/4 oz carrots, cut into matchsticks
200 g/7 oz bean sprouts
100 g/4 oz fresh spinach, chopped
1 small red chilli, chopped
1 tsp ground paprika
3 tbsp light soy sauce
salt and black pepper
4 tomato wedges
sliced cucumber

● Soak the rice vermicelli in warm water for 3 minutes or according to the instructions on the packet. Rinse and drain. Heat 2 tablespoons of the oil in a wok or frying pan, and stir fry the ginger and shallots for 30 seconds. Add the squid and stir until the squid turns white.
● Add the carrots, bean sprouts, spinach and chilli and stir for 1–2 minutes. Add the remaining tablespoon of oil, vermicelli, paprika, soy sauce and stir well.
● Taste and add the salt and black pepper if required. Put the vermicelli on to four plates and garnish with the tomato wedges and sliced cucumber. Serve at once.

fried flat rice noodles with beef and black bean sauce

Black bean sauce is just one of a number of end products that result from the fermentation of soya beans. Prepared with salt and spices, the black bean forms the basis of a very distinctive sauce to complement most meats. Here it is used with beef, but it makes an equally good companion to pork.

900 g/2 lb fresh flat rice noodles or 280 g/10 oz dried rice stick noodles
450 g/1 lb rump steak, sliced at a slant into bite-sized pieces
1 egg white
3 tbsp Chinese rice wine or dry sherry
4 tbsp light soy sauce
2 tsp cornflour
7 tbsp vegetable oil
2.5 cm/1 in fresh ginger, peeled and minced
3 cloves garlic, minced
2 spring onions, chopped
2 medium-sized onions, cut into bite-sized squares
1 large green pepper, cut into bite-sized squares
6 tbsp black bean sauce
2 tsp caster sugar

● Rinse fresh flat rice noodles with hot water, or soak dried noodles in warm water for 2–5 minutes. Rinse and drain.
● Marinate the beef with 1 tablespoon of the rice wine, 1 tablespoon of the soy sauce and the cornflour for 30 minutes.
● Heat 3 tablespoons of the oil in a wok or frying pan. Fry the beef for 2–3 minutes and set aside. Clean the wok.
● Heat 2 tablespoons of the oil in a wok and stir fry the ginger and garlic for 30 seconds. Add the spring onion, onion and green pepper and stir until the onion becomes transparent.
● Add the beef and noodles to the wok. Add the remaining oil, soy sauce and rice wine, the black bean sauce and the sugar. Stir well, until all the ingredients are thoroughly mixed. Divide the noodles on to four plates and serve.

Right

Fried Flat Rice Noodles with Beef and Black Bean Sauce

fried rice stick noodles with bean curd and black bean sauce

Tofu is prepared by cutting it into small cubes. Be careful when you do this as it is delicate stuff and prone to disintegrate if handled too roughly. Nutritious and healthy as it undoubtedly is, *tofu* will never win any awards for flavour, which is why its combination with the spicy, aromatic black bean sauce makes such a good pairing.

280 g/10 oz dried rice stick noodles
4 tbsp vegetable oil
350 g/12 oz bean curd (*tofu*), diced
2.5 cm/1 in fresh ginger, peeled and minced
2 cloves garlic, minced
½ green pepper, diced
½ red pepper, diced
½ yellow pepper, diced
5 spring onions, chopped
6 tbsp black bean sauce
3 tbsp light soy sauce
2 tbsp Chinese rice wine or dry sherry
2 tsp caster sugar

● Soak the rice stick noodles in warm water for 2–5 minutes, depending on the instructions on the packet. Rinse and drain.

● Heat 3 tablespoons of the oil in a wok or frying pan. Fry the bean curd until golden brown. Add the ginger and garlic and stir. Add the peppers and spring onion, and stir fry for 1–2 minutes.

● Add the remaining oil, noodles, black bean sauce, soy sauce, rice wine and sugar, then stir until the noodles are well coated with the sauce. Divide the noodles on to four plates and serve at once.

Right
Fried Rice Stick Noodles with Beancurd and Black Bean Sauce

spicy rice stick noodles with chicken

Authentic Thai spicy noodles are very hot indeed. I have altered the amount of green chilli used in this recipe to cool them down and save your taste buds! However, if you feel like increasing the spices, you can add more green chilli if you dare.

900 g/2 lb fresh flat rice noodles or 280 g/10 oz dried rice stick noodles
5 tbsp vegetable oil
2 cloves garlic, minced
4–6 small green chillies, chopped
225 g/8 oz boneless chicken breasts, sliced into bite-sized pieces
100 g/4 oz frozen green beans, halved
100 g/4 oz mustard greens or fresh spinach
16 tinned baby corn, each cut diagonally into 3 pieces
4 tbsp fish sauce (nam pla)
2 tbsp dark soy sauce
2 tbsp light soy sauce
1 tbsp palm or brown sugar
2 small tomatoes, halved

● If you use fresh noodles, just rinse with warm water. Soak dried rice noodles in warm water for 2–5 minutes or according to the instructions on the packet. Rinse and drain.

● Heat 3 tablespoons of the oil in a wok or frying pan until very hot. Stir fry the garlic and green chilli for 30 seconds, then add the chicken and fry for about 3 minutes.

● Add the green beans, mustard greens or spinach and baby corn, stirring for 1–2 minutes. Add the remaining oil and the rice noodles and stir. Then add fish sauce, soy sauce and sugar and stir well.

● Garnish with tomatoes and serve at once.

Thai fried rice stick noodles
pad thai

The most widely eaten and best known of all the noodle dishes of Thailand. Like all the best noodle dishes, pad thai is simply prepared and ready in minutes. The key to a tasty pad thai lies in the use of salty dried shrimps and roasted peanuts. You can adjust the amount of chilli used depending on your liking for spiciness.

280 g/10 oz dried rice stick noodles
12 king or large prawns with tails, peeled and deveined
5 tbsp vegetable oil
3 cloves garlic, minced
4 shallots, sliced
2 eggs, beaten
2 tbsp roast peanuts, crushed
3–4 small green chillies, chopped
2 tbsp dried shrimps, chopped
2 spring onions, chopped
200 g/7 oz bean sprouts
2½ tbsp palm or brown sugar
6 tbsp fish sauce (nam pla)
120 ml/4 fl oz freshly squeezed lemon juice
coriander leaves
4 lime wedges
For the prawn marinade:
1 tsp freshly squeezed lemon juice
1 tsp fish sauce (nam pla)
½ tsp palm or brown sugar

● Soak the rice stick noodles in warm water for 2–5 minutes or according to the instructions on the packet. Rinse and drain.

● Marinate the prawns in the lemon juice, fish sauce and sugar for at least 15 minutes.

● Heat 2 tablespoons of the oil in a wok or frying pan, and stir fry the garlic and shallots for 30 seconds. Make a well in the centre and add the eggs, then lightly scramble without incorporating the garlic and shallots.

● Add the peanuts, chillies, dried shrimps, spring onion and bean sprouts, and stir.

● Add another 2 tablespoons of oil and the noodles and stir. Add the sugar, fish sauce and lemon juice, then stir until the noodles are well coated.

● Quickly heat the remaining tablespoon of oil in the wok and fry the prawns thoroughly. Put the noodles on to four plates. Lay the prawns on top and garnish with coriander and lime wedges. Serve at once.

Right
Thai Fried Rice Stick Noodles

rice stick noodles with pork and prawns

This dish contains the three foundations of Thai flavouring: garlic, shallots and chillies. Thai garlic tends to be small compared to its European counterpart, so if the cloves you have are on the large side, use one instead of the two listed below.

280 g/10 oz dried rice stick noodles
5 tbsp vegetable oil
2 cloves garlic, minced
3 shallots, chopped
225 g/8 oz lean pork, sliced into small pieces
100 g/4 oz peeled prawns
4–6 small green chillies, chopped
200 g/7 oz bean sprouts
8 tinned baby corn, cut diagonally into bite-sized pieces
3 sticks celery, cut diagonally into bite-sized pieces
2 eggs, beaten
2½ tbsp palm or brown sugar
3½ tbsp tomato ketchup
6 tbsp fish sauce (nam pla)
120 ml/4 fl oz freshly squeezed lemon juice
coriander leaves
4 lime wedges

● Soak the rice stick noodles in warm water for 2–5 minutes or according to the instructions on the packet. Rinse and drain.
● Heat 3 tablespoons of the oil in a wok or frying pan and stir fry the garlic and shallots for 30 seconds. Add the pork and fry for about 3 minutes. Add the prawns and green chilli, stirring for

another minute, then add the bean sprouts, baby corn and celery and fry for another 2 minutes.
● Make a well in the centre, then pour in the egg and scramble quickly. Add the remaining oil and the rice stick noodles, then stir. Add the sugar, tomato ketchup, fish sauce and lemon juice and stir well.
● Divide the noodles onto four plates and garnish with the coriander and lime wedges.

fried rice noodles with coconut sauce

The coconut and its parent palm have a hallowed place in the Thai psyche. The coconut itself has a wide variety of culinary uses while the palm is employed to make furniture, toys and musical instruments. Tinned coconut milk varies in its consistency depending on the brand. A thicker product produces the richest, smoothest flavour. Remember to shake the tin well before opening.

280 g/10 oz dried rice stick noodles
3 tbsp vegetable oil
2 cloves garlic, minced
3 shallots, chopped
400 g/14 oz rump steak, thinly sliced
16 tinned baby corn, cut diagonally
4 spring onions, chopped
2 sticks celery, chopped
200 g/7 oz bean sprouts
375 ml/13 fl oz tinned coconut milk
2 tsp palm or brown sugar
4 tbsp fish sauce (nam pla)
3 tbsp freshly squeezed lemon juice
1 tbsp Thai red curry paste
coriander leaves

● Soak the rice stick noodles in warm water for 2–5 minutes or follow the instructions on the packet. Rinse and drain.
● Heat the oil in a wok or frying pan, stir fry the garlic and shallots for 30 seconds. Add the beef and stir fry for about 3 minutes, before adding the baby corn, spring onion, celery and bean sprouts.
● Add the coconut milk, sugar, fish sauce, lemon juice and curry paste and stir well until the sauce is absorbed into the noodles.
● Put the noodles on to four plates, sprinkle with coriander leaves and serve at once.

fried bean thread noodles with bean curd

Bean curd is a favourite constituent of Thai cooking. This dish features fried bean curd. Like all other types of bean curd, it is best to use what you buy in one go as it quickly deteriorates even if refrigerated.

225 g/8 oz bean thread noodles
4 tbsp vegetable oil
280 g/10 oz bean curd (*tofu*),
  diced
3 cloves garlic, minced
4 shallots, minced
200 g/7 oz bean sprouts
100 g/4 oz frozen green beans,
  halved
2 spring onions, chopped
2 tbsp roast peanuts, crushed
2 tbsp dried shrimps, chopped
3–5 small green chillies,
  chopped
2½ tbsp palm or brown sugar
6 tbsp fish sauce (*nam pla*)
120 ml/4 fl oz freshly squeezed
  lemon juice
For the garnish:
2 tbsp crispy onion (*see glossary*)
coriander leaves
1 medium red chilli, sliced
4 slices lime

● Soak the bean thread noodles in boiling water for 5 minutes. Rinse under cold water and drain. Heat half the oil in a wok or frying pan and fry the bean curd until golden brown. Drain on absorbent paper.

● Add the remaining oil to the wok, then fry the garlic and shallots for about 30 seconds. Add the bean sprouts, green beans and spring onions and stir well.

● Add the bean thread noodles, bean curd, crushed peanuts, dried shrimps and green chilli and stir. Season with the sugar, fish sauce and lemon juice, stirring again.

● Divide the noodles on to four plates. Sprinkle with the crispy onions, coriander leaves, red chilli and garnish with a slice of lime. Serve at once.

Left
Fried Bean Thread Noodles with Beancurd

[105]

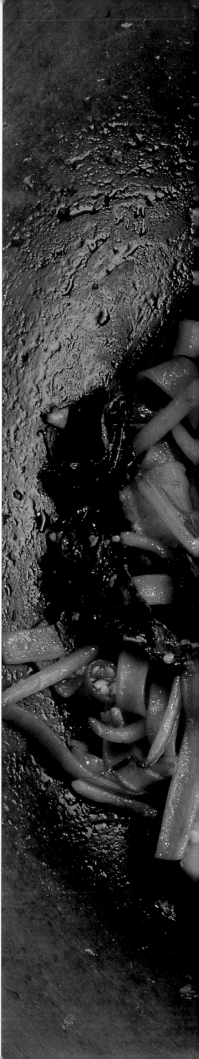

Malaysian fried rice noodles

kway teow

If you are ever lucky enough to visit Malaysia, you will find this dish being sold in restaurants and from roadside stalls wherever you go. The fish balls in this recipe are not available at supermarkets but you should be able to pick them up at oriental food stores.

900 g/2 lb fresh flat rice noodles
  or 280 g/10 oz dried rice stick
  noodles
5 tbsp vegetable oil
2 cloves garlic, minced
1 cm/½ in ginger, peeled and
  minced
150 g/6 oz boneless belly of
  pork or chicken breasts,
  skinned and thinly sliced
2 small red chillies, chopped
16 tiger or large prawns with
  tails, peeled and deveined
8 fish balls, sliced or seafood
  sticks
225 g/8 oz bean sprouts
100 g/4 oz fresh spinach
2 eggs, beaten
1 tsp caster sugar
3 tbsp light soy sauce
3 tbsp dark soy sauce
salt and black pepper

● Rinse the fresh flat rice noodles with warm water or soak the dried rice stick noodles in warm water for 2–5 minutes. Rinse and drain.

● Heat 3 tablespoons of the oil in a wok or frying pan until very hot. Stir fry the garlic and ginger for 30 seconds. Add the pork and fry for about 3 minutes. Add the chilli and prawns, then stir for about 1 minute. Add the sliced fish balls, bean sprouts and spinach and stir again for about 1 minute.

● Make a well in the centre, then add the egg. Scramble quickly. Add the remaining oil, and the rice noodles, sugar and soy sauce, then stir well. Taste and add the salt and black pepper. Put on to four plates and serve immediately.

Right
*Malaysian
Fried Rice
Noodles*

noodles with toppings

The concept of this style of noodles is similar to the thinking behind Italian pasta. While you prepare the noodles, you can make the toppings. There are two ways of preparing noodles. They can be boiled like spaghetti, or deep fried to make them crispy – egg noodles and rice vermicelli are the noodles most commonly deep fried.

soft noodles with vegetable and peanut sauce

gado gado

Gado gado is one of the most famous and commonly eaten Indonesian dishes, comprising vegetables in a peanut sauce. Normally it is served as a salad but it also makes a great noodle topping!

80 g/3 oz green cabbage, sliced
200 g/7 oz bean sprouts
80 g/3 oz green beans
100 g/4 oz carrots, cut into matchsticks
400 g/14 oz fresh or 280 g/10 oz dried thin egg noodles
1 tbsp sesame oil
For the peanut sauce:
1 tbsp vegetable oil
1 clove garlic, minced
1 shallot, minced
½ tsp chilli powder
500 ml/18 fl oz water
1 tbsp light brown sugar
8 tbsp crunchy peanut butter
a pinch of salt
juice of ½ a lemon

● Heat the oil in a frying pan and stir fry the garlic and shallot for 1 minute or until softened. Add the chilli powder, water, sugar and peanut butter and stir well. Add the salt and lemon juice, stirring again.

● Boil water in a pan and blanch the cabbage, bean sprouts, green beans and carrots for 2–3 minutes. Drain well.

● Boil more water in the pan and cook the egg noodles for 3 minutes. Rinse, drain and toss with the sesame oil. Divide them on to four plates.

● Pile the vegetables on the noodles and pour the peanut sauce over. Serve at once.

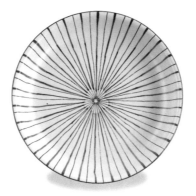

soft egg noodles with minced pork sauce

Toban djan is a fiery Chinese chilli bean sauce available from most Chinese or oriental stores and in a growing number of supermarkets. Here, the power of the chilli sauce is tempered by the addition of yellow bean sauce leaving the dish pleasantly spicy rather than breathtakingly hot.

280 g/10 oz dried or 400 g/14 oz fresh thin egg noodles
2 tsp sesame oil
For the sauce:
2 tbsp vegetable oil
1 large clove garlic, minced
1 cm/½ in fresh ginger, peeled and minced
2 spring onions, chopped
450 g/1 lb minced pork
3 tbsp yellow bean sauce
1 tbsp chilli bean sauce (*toban djan*)
2 tbsp Chinese rice wine or dry sherry
2 tbsp dark soy sauce
450 ml/¾ pt chicken stock (*see page 25*) mixed to a paste with 2 tbsp cornflour
salt and black pepper

● Cook the egg noodles in plenty of boiling water for 3 minutes. Rinse and drain. Toss in the sesame oil and divide into four servings.

● Heat the vegetable oil in a pan and stir fry the garlic, ginger and spring onion for 30 seconds. Add the minced pork and fry for 3–4 minutes.

● Add the yellow bean sauce, chilli sauce, rice wine and soy sauce and stir for one minute.

● Add the mixture of stock and cornflour and stir until the sauce thickens. Season with salt and black pepper to taste.

● Pour the sauce over the noodles and serve immediately.

Right
Soft Egg Noodles with Minced Pork Sauce

fried egg noodles with seafood sauce

If you have a taste for slightly richer flavours, try adding eight abalone to the ingredients.

280 g/10 oz dried egg noodles
4 tbsp vegetable oil
1 tbsp sesame oil
2.5 cm/1 in fresh ginger, peeled and minced
2 cloves garlic, minced
280 g/10 oz squid, cleaned
150 g/6 oz peeled tiger prawns
4 fish balls, sliced or seafood sticks
250 g/9 oz Chinese cabbage, cut into bite-sized squares
salt and white pepper
600 ml/1 pt chicken or vegetable stock
 (see pages 25–26)
1 tbsp Chinese rice wine or dry sherry
3 tbsp cornflour
4 tbsp water

● Cook the egg noodles in boiling water for 3 minutes. Rinse and drain. Heat 1 tbsp of the vegetable oil and sesame oil in a wok or frying pan. Stir fry the noodles and put on four plates.
● Heat the remaining vegetable oil in the wok, and stir fry the ginger and garlic for 30 seconds. Add the squid and prawns, stirring for 1–2 minutes or until the squid is cooked thoroughly.
● Add the slices of fish ball and Chinese cabbage, sprinkle with salt and white pepper and stir. Add the stock and rice wine and bring to the boil. Simmer for 1–2 minutes.
● Combine the cornflour and water and add to thicken the sauce. Pour the sauce over the noodles and serve.

fried egg noodles with pork and aubergine sauce

Oyster sauce is a frequently used Chinese flavouring. The surprising thing about oyster sauce is that you would be hard put to find any trace of fishiness in its flavour. It will last for long periods if kept refrigerated and is widely available from supermarkets.

400 g/14 oz fresh or 280 g/10 oz dried medium egg noodles
2 tbsp sesame oil
For the sauce:
280 g/10 oz boneless belly of pork, skinned and thinly sliced
2½ tbsp light soy sauce
2½ tbsp Chinese rice wine or dry sherry
4 tbsp cornflour
4 tbsp vegetable oil
2.5 cm/1 in fresh ginger, peeled and minced
2 cloves garlic, minced
300 g/11 oz aubergine, sliced into bite-sized pieces and soaked in water
100 g/4 oz carrots, sliced
16 tinned straw mushrooms, halved
2 spring onions, chopped into 2.5 cm/1 in lengths
black pepper
600 ml/1 pt chicken stock
 (see page 25)
2 tbsp oyster sauce
1 tsp caster sugar
4 tbsp water

● Marinate the pork in 1 tablespoon each of soy sauce, rice wine and cornflour. Set aside for 30 minutes, then heat 1 tbsp of the vegetable oil in a wok or frying pan and fry the pork for about 3 minutes until lightly browned. Clean the wok.
● Heat the rest of the vegetable oil in the wok until very hot and stir-fry the ginger and garlic for 30 seconds. Add the drained aubergine and carrots and stir-fry for a further 1–2 minutes. Add the pork, mushrooms and spring onions, sprinkle over the black pepper and stir.
● Add the chicken stock, rice wine, oyster sauce, soy sauce and sugar and bring to the boil, simmering for 1 minute. Dissolve the cornflour in the water and add to thicken the sauce.
● Boil the egg noodles in plenty of water for 4 minutes. Rinse under running water and drain. Heat the sesame oil in a wok, add the noodles and quickly stir fry.
● Divide the egg noodles on to four plates, pour the pork and aubergine sauce over, then serve at once.

Right

Fried Egg Noodles with Pork and Aubergine

shredded beef and yellow bean sauce on pan-fried egg noodles

Yellow bean sauce is available in two varieties, one using whole beans, which has to be roughly crushed before use, and the other puréed. The texture differs but the taste is identical. You can use either in this dish.

450 g/1 lb rump steak, shredded
1 tbsp light soy sauce
1 tbsp Chinese rice wine or dry
   sherry
1 tbsp cornflour
400 g/14 oz fresh or 280 g/10 oz
   dried thin egg noodles
4 tbsp vegetable oil
For the sauce:
2 tbsp vegetable oil
1 cm/½ in fresh ginger, peeled
   and minced
10 cm/4 in leek, cut in half and
   shredded
200 g/7 oz bean sprouts
1 small green pepper, sliced
salt and black pepper
400 ml/14 fl oz chicken stock
   (see page 25)
6 tbsp whole or puréed yellow
   bean sauce
1 tbsp light soy sauce
2 tbsp cornflour
3 tbsp water

● Marinate the beef in the soy sauce, rice wine and cornflour for 30 minutes.
● Meanwhile, cook the egg noodles in a pan of boiling water for 3 minutes. Rinse, drain and divide into four. Heat 1 tablespoon of oil in a wok or frying pan. Take one quarter of the noodles and fry them like a pancake. Press the noodles to form a round and when they have started to turn golden in colour, turn to fry on the other side. Remove to a chopping board and cut twice in a criss-cross pattern to make the noodles easier to eat. Put the noodles on an individual plate. Repeat the process with the other three portions.
● To make the sauce, heat 2 tablespoons of oil in the wok or frying pan and fry the ginger for 30 seconds. Add the leek, beans prouts and green pepper, stirring each ingredient as you add it. Sprinkle with salt and black pepper.
● Add the stock, yellow bean sauce and soy sauce, and bring to the boil. Dissolve the cornflour in water, then add to thicken the sauce. Pour the sauce over the noodles before serving.

Malaysian egg noodles with chicken and prawns

A Malaysian Chinese dish with a characteristic savoury sauce. A typical feature of Malaysian and Singaporean cookery is the frequent use of egg, as in this dish, in which strands of beaten egg are stirred into the sauce.

400 g/14 oz fresh or 280 g/10 oz
   dried thin egg noodles
2 tbsp sesame oil
4 tbsp vegetable oil
2 cloves garlic, minced
100 g/4 oz boneless chicken
   breasts, sliced into bite-sized
   pieces
100 g/4 oz peeled prawns
4 fish balls, sliced
225 g/8 oz bean sprouts
100 g/4 oz mustard greens or
   fresh spinach
1 tsp light soy sauce
1 tsp salt
white pepper
½ tsp caster sugar
600 ml/1 pt chicken stock
   (see page 25)
3 tbsp cornflour
4 tbsp water
2 eggs, beaten

● Boil plenty of water in a pan and add the egg noodles. Cook for 3 minutes and rinse under cold water and drain. Heat the sesame oil in a wok or frying pan and fry the noodles. Then divide on to four plates.
● Heat the vegetable oil in a wok or frying pan until very hot. Fry the garlic for 30 seconds. Add the chicken and fry for 2–3 minutes. Add the prawns and stir, then add the fish balls, bean sprouts and spinach or greens, stirring for 2–3 minutes.
● Add the soy sauce, salt, pepper, sugar and chicken stock; bring to the boil. Dissolve the cornflour in water, then add to thicken the sauce. When the sauce returns to the boil, stir in the beaten egg and wait for the egg strands to float up to the surface. Pour the sauce over the noodles and serve.

Right
Malaysian Egg Noodles with Chicken and Prawns

sweet and sour fish on pan-fried egg noodles

Sweet and sour fish has never quite gained the same kind of popularity as sweet and sour pork, though it is every bit as good to eat and makes an especially good noodle topping.

vegetable oil for deep frying
2 tbsp cornflour
I egg, beaten
I tsp water
450 g/I lb cod or haddock
  steaks, cut into bite-sized
  pieces
280 g/10 oz dried or 400 g/14 oz
  fresh thin egg noodles
4 tbsp vegetable oil
For the sauce:
I tbsp sesame oil
2 tbsp vegetable oil
I medium-sized onion, cut into
  bite-sized squares
I red pepper, cut into bite-sized
  squares
50 g/2 oz frozen green peas
100 g/4 oz tinned bamboo
  shoots, cut into halves
10 *shiitake* mushrooms,
  quartered
½ tsp chilli powder
600 ml/I pt chicken stock
  (see page 25)
2⅔ tbsp caster sugar
120 ml/4 fl oz tomato ketchup
4 tsp light soy sauce
4 tbsp Chinese rice wine or dry
  sherry
4 tbsp vinegar
salt and black pepper
3 tbsp cornflour
4 tbsp water

● Heat the oil in a pan to 180°C/350°F. Meanwhile, mix the cornflour, egg and water together and dip the fish in the mixture. Deep fry for about 2 minutes or until golden brown.

● Cook the egg noodles in plenty of boiling water for 3 minutes. Rinse under running water, drain well and divide into four. Heat I tablespoon of oil in a wok or frying pan. Add a portion of noodles and press down lightly. Fry until lightly browned, then turn the noodles over, press down lightly and fry until the other side turns golden brown.

● Put the pan-fried noodles on a chopping board, make a criss-cross pattern of cuts and move on to an individual plate. Repeat the process for the other three portions.

● Heat I tbsp sesame oil and 2 tbsp vegetable oil in the wok or frying pan until very hot. Stir fry the onion, red pepper and peas for 2 minutes. Add the bamboo shoots and *shiitake* mushrooms and sprinkle over the chilli powder. Stir fry for another 2 minutes.

● Add the chicken stock, sugar, tomato ketchup, soy sauce and rice wine and bring to the boil. Add the vinegar and season with salt and black pepper.

● Dissolve the cornflour in the water and add to thicken the sauce. Add the fish and stir gently. Pour the sweet and sour fish over the noodles. Serve immediately.

crab meat sauce on pan-fried egg noodles

280 g/10 oz dried or 400 g/14 oz
  fresh medium egg noodles
4 tbsp vegetable oil
For the crab meat sauce:
2 tbsp vegetable oil
I clove garlic, minced
I cm/½ in fresh ginger, peeled
  and minced
10 *shiitake* mushrooms, sliced
150 g/6 oz tinned bamboo
  shoots, sliced into matchsticks
4 spring onions, chopped
350 g/12 oz tinned crab meat
600 ml/I pt water
4 tsp light soy sauce
salt and black pepper
3 tbsp cornflour
4 tbsp water

● Cook the egg noodles in plenty of water for 4 minutes. Rinse, drain well and divide into four. Heat I tablespoon of oil in a wok or frying pan until very hot. Press one portion of the egg noodles down lightly into the pan and fry until lightly browned on both sides. Place on a chopping board and cut a criss-cross pattern. Remove to a plate. Repeat with the three remaining portions.

● Heat two tablespoons of oil in the cleaned wok. Fry the garlic and ginger for 30 seconds. Add the *shiitake* mushrooms, bamboo shoots and spring onions and stir fry for I–2 minutes. Add the crab meat, water and soy sauce and season. Bring to the boil and simmer for I minute.

● Dissolve the cornflour in the water and add to thicken the sauce. Stir. Pour the sauce over the noodles and serve.

Right

Crab Meat Sauce on Pan-fried Egg Noodles

Thai sweet crispy rice vermicelli

mee krob

Mee krob requires a little more time than most noodle dishes but is well worth the extra effort. It is essential that the dish is served as soon as it is ready as the vermicelli will become mushy if left for very long.

60 g/2 oz rice vermicelli, slightly crushed
vegetable oil for deep frying
1 tbsp vegetable oil
2 cloves garlic, minced
2 shallots, minced
12 tiger prawns with tails, peeled and deveined
4 tbsp raw cashew nuts
For the sauce:
3 tbsp palm or brown sugar
2 tbsp freshly squeezed lemon juice
1 tsp vinegar
1 tsp light soy sauce
2 tbsp tomato ketchup
½ tsp chilli powder
For the garnish:
2 lettuce leaves, halved
coriander leaves
2 small tomato wedges

● Heat the oil in a wok or saucepan to 180°C/350°F. Deep fry the vermicelli for a few seconds until they puff up and become white. Drain on absorbent paper.

● Heat the oil in the wok or frying pan. Add the garlic and shallots and stir. Add the tiger prawns and cashew nuts and stir fry for around 2 minutes.

● Add the sugar, lemon juice, vinegar, soy sauce, ketchup and chilli powder, and simmer until the sauce thickens. Take out the prawns and set aside.

● Add the crispy vermicelli and coat with the sauce. Put the vermicelli on a bed of lettuce on four plates. Garnish each serving with three prawns, coriander and tomato wedges. Serve.

crispy egg noodles with pork sauce

Deep-fried noodles might seem like a strange idea, but, in fact, are very popular throughout Asia, and makes a crunchy and refreshing alternative to boiled noodles.

225 g/8 oz dried thin egg noodles
vegetable oil for deep frying
For the sauce:
225 g/8 oz lean pork, sliced on the slant into bite-sized pieces
1 tbsp light soy sauce
4 tbsp cornflour
8 large dried *shiitake* mushrooms, rinsed
4 tbsp vegetable oil
2.5 cm/1 in fresh ginger, peeled and minced
2 cloves garlic, minced
1 medium-sized onion, cut into bite-sized squares
100 g/4 oz carrots, thinly sliced

225 g/8 oz Chinese cabbage, cut into bite-sized squares
salt and black pepper
600 ml/1 pt chicken stock
 (see page 25)
2 tbsp Chinese rice wine or dry sherry
2 tsp caster sugar
4 tbsp water

● Boil plenty of water in a saucepan and cook the noodles for 3 minutes. Rinse and drain. Separate and spread the noodles on a tray to dry.

● Heat a wok or saucepan a quarter full of oil and heat to 180°C/350°F. Deep fry the egg noodles in small batches until golden and crispy. Drain on absorbent paper.

● Put the pork, soy sauce and 1 tablespoon of the cornflour in a bowl, mix and leave for 15 minutes. Soak the *shiitake* mushrooms in 225 ml/8 fl oz hot water for 15 minutes, then remove and quarter. Retain the water. Heat 2 tablespoons of the oil in a wok or frying pan and fry the pork for about 3 minutes. Set aside and clean the pan.

● Heat the remaining oil in the wok and fry the ginger and garlic for 30 seconds, before adding the carrots, shiitake mushrooms and chinese cabbages. Stir fry for 2–3 minutes. Add the meat and season with salt and pepper and stir.

● Add the water used to soak the mushrooms, chicken stock, rice wine and sugar and bring to the boil. Check the saltiness. Dissolve the cornflour in the water and add to thicken the sauce. Crush the crispy noodles lightly then put on to four plates. Pour the sauce over and serve at once.

Right

Crispy Egg Noodles with Pork Sauce

crispy egg noodles with bean curd and vegetable sauce

This dish is also suitable for vegetarians as I have not used chicken stock. The strong scent of the *shiitake* mushrooms flavours the water which can be used to add extra aroma to the sauce.

225 g/8 oz dried thin egg noodles
vegetable oil for deep frying
For the sauce:
2 tbsp vegetable oil
675 g/1½ lb bean curd (tofu)
1 tbsp sesame oil
2.5 cm/1 in fresh ginger, peeled and minced
2 cloves garlic, minced
8 dried *shiitake* mushrooms, rinsed
100 g/4 oz tinned bamboo shoots
4 tbsp frozen green peas
150 g/6 oz leek, sliced
4 tsp dark soy sauce
4 tsp light soy sauce
4 tsp yellow bean sauce
½ tsp chilli bean sauce (toban djan)
salt and black pepper
3 tbsp cornflour mixed with 4 tbsp water

● Cook the egg noodles in a pan of boiling water for 3 minutes. Rinse and drain well. Separate and spread the noodles on a tray to dry. Meanwhile, soak the *shiitake* mushrooms in hot water for 20 minutes, then cut into bite-sized pieces. Retain the water for the stock.

● Fill a wok or pan a quarter full with vegetable oil and heat to 180°C/350°F. Deep fry the egg noodles in small batches until golden and crispy. Drain on absorbent paper and crush lightly.
● Heat 1 tablespoon of the vegetable oil in the wok or frying pan, and fry the bean curd until lightly browned. Drain on absorbent paper and clean the wok.
● Heat the remaining tablespoon of vegetable oil and the sesame oil in the wok or pan. Stir fry the ginger and garlic for 30 seconds, add the mushrooms, bamboo shoots, peas and leek and stir fry.
● Make up the soaking water from the mushrooms to 600 ml/1 pt, then pour into the wok. Add the soy sauce, yellow bean sauce and chilli bean sauce and bring to the boil. Season with salt and black pepper if required. Add the cornflour paste to thicken the sauce. Simmer gently for 1 minute.
● Place the crispy egg noodles on to four plates. Pour the sauce over, then serve at once.

chicken and red pepper in egg noodle basket

Noodle baskets are a Chinese innovation that appeal as much to the eyes as to the taste buds. You will need two small sieves about 12 cm/5 in across. I find this recipe works best with thinner noodles, and the oil needs to be hot to get nice crisp golden baskets. This recipe makes six baskets which can be presented as a main dish or as a starter with less filling.

200 g/7 oz dried thin egg noodles
vegetable oil for deep frying
For the filling:
6 tbsp vegetable oil
450 g/1 lb boneless chicken breasts, sliced diagonally into bite-sized pieces
salt and black pepper
3 tbsp cornflour
4 cloves garlic, minced
4 cm/1½ in fresh ginger, peeled and minced
100 g/4 oz tinned bamboo shoots, sliced into matchsticks
⅔ red pepper, diced
4 spring onions, chopped
For the sauce:
150 ml/¼ pt chicken stock (see page 25)
1 tbsp Chinese rice wine or dry sherry
1 tbsp light soy sauce
2 tsp dark soy sauce
4 tsp tomato ketchup
½ tsp caster sugar
salt and black pepper
½ tbsp cornflour
2 tsp water

● Boil the egg noodles for 3 minutes. Rinse with water, drain, separate and dry on a tray lined with kitchen towel.

● Heat the oil in a deep pan to 180°C/350°F. Oil the sieves, one on the inside, the other on the outside. Line one sieve with egg noodles and press down lightly the other sieve to sandwich them. Carefully deep fry the noodles with the two sieves holding them together until crispy and golden, about 3–4 minutes. Remove the noodle basket, taking care not to break it. Create 5 more baskets in the same way.

● Heat 4 tbsp of oil in a wok or frying pan. Sprinkle the chicken with the salt and pepper, then coat with the cornflour. Shallow fry the chicken for 3–4 minutes or until golden brown. Drain on absorbent paper.

● Heat the remaining 2 tablespoons of oil in the wok, stir fry the garlic and ginger, then add the bamboo, red pepper and onion. Stir well. Add the chicken stock, rice wine, soy sauce, ketchup and caster sugar, bring to the boil and season if required.

● Combine the cornflour and water and add to thicken the sauce. Return the chicken to the pan and stir. Place the noodle baskets on 6 plates and put the chicken in them. Serve at once.

Left

Chicken and Red Pepper in Egg Noodle Basket

crispy egg noodles with chicken and bean sprout sauce

Take care when preparing the noodles for this dish, as the oil may boil over if an excessive amount is used. The best and safest method is to use a wok rather than a frying pan.

**225 g/8 oz dried medium egg
    noodles**
vegetable oil for deep frying
1 egg white
2 tsp cornflour
6 tbsp vegetable oil
**280 g/10 oz boneless chicken
    breasts, shredded**
For the sauce:
1 tbsp sesame oil
2 cloves garlic, minced
**2.5 cm/1 in fresh ginger, peeled
    and minced**
400 g/14 oz bean sprouts
**15 tinned straw mushrooms,
    halved**
4 spring onions, chopped
600 ml/1 pt chicken stock
    (see page 25)
2 tsp light soy sauce
**2 tbsp Chinese rice wine or dry
    sherry**
salt and black pepper
3 tbsp cornflour
4 tbsp water

● Boil plenty of water in a pan and cook the noodles for 4 minutes. Rinse and drain. Separate and spread the noodles on a tray to dry.

● Fill a saucepan or wok quarter full of oil and heat to 180°C/350°F. Deep fry the noodles in small batches until golden and crispy. Drain on absorbent paper. Crush the noodles lightly to make them easier to handle and divide on to three plates.

● Mix the egg white and 2 tsp of cornflour. Heat 5 tablespoons of the vegetable oil in the wok or frying pan. Coat the chicken with the cornflour mixture, then shallow fry until golden brown. Discard the oil and clean the wok.

● Heat the remaining tablespoon of vegetable oil and the sesame oil in the wok until very hot. Stir fry the garlic and ginger for 30 seconds. Add the bean sprouts, mushrooms and spring onion and stir fry for 2 minutes.

● Return the chicken to the wok, then add the stock, soy sauce, rice wine. Season with salt and black pepper. Bring to the boil and simmer for 1–2 minutes.

● Dissolve the cornflour in the water, then add to thicken the sauce. Pour the sauce over the noodles just prior to eating.

crispy rice vermicelli with shredded chicken

You will be surprised at the rapid expansion of the vermicelli the first time you try this dish. The key is to deep fry it in small amounts to prevent it from overflowing from your wok or pan. The noodles are ready when they have lost their transparency and have turned white.

100 g/4 oz rice vermicelli
vegetable oil for deep frying
For the sauce:
**450 g/1 lb boneless chicken
    breasts, shredded**
2 tbsp light soy sauce
**2 tbsp Chinese rice wine or dry
    sherry**
3 tbsp cornflour
4 tbsp vegetable oil
**2.5 cm/1 in fresh ginger, peeled
    and minced**
8 *shiitake* mushrooms, shredded
12 water chestnuts, sliced
**4 spring onions, chopped into
    2.5 cm/1 in lengths**
salt and black pepper
450 ml/¾ pt chicken stock
    (see page 25)
1 tsp sesame oil
1 tbsp tomato ketchup
½ tsp sugar
3 tbsp water
**6 lettuce leaves, rinsed and
    quartered**

● Fill a wok or saucepan a quarter full of vegetable oil and heat to 180°C/350°F. Deep fry the rice vermicelli in small batches at a time. It will puff up in seconds. Drain on absorbent paper.

● Marinate the chicken in 1 table-spoon each of the soy sauce, rice wine and cornflour for 30 minutes. Heat 2 tbsp of oil in a wok or frying pan and fry the chicken for 3–4 minutes. Set aside and clean the wok.

● Heat the remaining 2 tablespoons of the vegetable oil in the wok. Add the ginger and stir fry for 30 seconds. Add the *shiitake* mushrooms, water chestnuts, spring onion and chicken, sprinkle with salt and pepper, then stir fry for 1–2 minutes.

● Add the chicken stock, sesame oil, tomato ketchup, sugar and remaining soy sauce and rice wine, and bring to the boil. Combine the remaining cornflour and water, then add to thicken the sauce. Stir well.

● To serve, pile the lettuce leaves on to a small plate. Put the crispy vermicelli on to four individual plates and pour the chicken sauce over. When you eat, take one lettuce leaf and wrap some noodles and chicken sauce together in a bundle and pop into your mouth.

Right

Crispy Rice Vermicelli with Shredded Chicken

beef and celery on crispy vermicelli

The steak used in this dish should be quite lean and cut small enough for it to absorb the flavours of the marinade, which contains vinegar to soften the meat.

450 g/1 lb rump steak, sliced
** diagonally into bite-sized**
** pieces**
1 tsp vinegar
2 tsp light soy sauce
1 egg white
125 g/5 oz rice vermicelli
vegetable oil for deep frying
4 tbsp vegetable oil
2 cloves garlic, minced
2.5 cm/1 in fresh ginger, peeled
** and minced**
3 spring onions, chopped
8 sticks celery, sliced diagonally
100 g/4 oz tinned bamboo
** shoots**
For the sauce:
450 ml/¾ pt chicken stock
** (see page 25)**
1 tbsp light soy sauce
1 tbsp Chinese rice wine or dry
** sherry**
2 tsp oyster sauce
2 tbsp cornflour mixed to a
** paste with 3 tbsp water**

- Marinate the beef in the vinegar, soy sauce and egg white for 30 minutes.
- Fill a wok or saucepan a quarter full of oil and heat to 180°C/350°F. Deep fry the vermicelli for a few seconds in small batches until they puff up. Drain on absorbent paper, then crush lightly and arrange on four plates.
- Heat 2 tablespoons of the oil in a wok or frying pan. Stir fry the beef until golden brown. Clean the pan.

- Heat the remaining 2 tablespoons of the oil in the wok. Stir fry the garlic, ginger, spring onion, celery and bamboo shoots for 2 minutes. Return the beef to the pan and stir well.
- Add the chicken stock, soy sauce, rice wine and oyster sauce and heat for 2 minutes. Stir in the combined cornflour paste to thicken the sauce. Pour the sauce over the crispy vermicelli and serve immediately.

crispy vermicelli with chicken and mango

A modern Chinese dish which looks set to become a great favourite. Fried vermicelli must be eaten as quickly as possible once it is ready.

125 g/5 oz rice vermicelli
vegetable oil for deep frying
1 egg white
3⅔ tbsp cornflour
450 g/1 lb boneless chicken
** breasts, sliced into bite-sized**
** pieces**
salt and black pepper
4 tbsp vegetable oil
2 cloves garlic, minced
2.5 cm/1 in fresh ginger, peeled
** and minced**
3 sticks celery, sliced diagonally
1 medium-sized onion, cubed
1 mango, cut into bite-sized
** pieces**
600 ml/1 pt chicken stock
** (see page 25)**
2 tbsp Chinese rice wine or dry
** sherry**
3 tbsp light soy sauce
2½ tbsp caster sugar
4 tbsp water

- Fill a wok or saucepan a quarter full of oil and heat to 180°C/350°F. Deep fry the vermicelli in small batches only a few seconds until they turn white. Drain on absorbent paper.
- Mix the egg white and 2 teaspoons of the cornflour in a bowl. Sprinkle the chicken with salt and black pepper and coat with the cornflour mixture.
- Heat 2 tablespoons of the oil in a wok or frying pan until very hot. Fry the chicken for about 2 minutes. When finished, discard the oil and clean the pan.
- Heat the remaining 2 tablespoons of oil in the wok. Stir fry the garlic and ginger for 30 seconds before adding the celery, onion and chicken. Stir fry for 2–3 minutes.
- Add the chicken stock, rice wine, soy sauce and sugar, and bring to the boil. Add the mango, season with salt and black pepper and simmer for 1–2 minutes. Combine the remaining cornflour with the water and add to thicken the sauce.
- Divide the crispy vermicelli on to four plates and lightly crush. Pour the sauce over prior to eating.

Right

Crispy Vermicelli with Chicken and Mango

sweet and sour pork on crispy vermicelli

Perhaps the most popular Chinese dish in the west. It is equally at home with noodles as with rice.

125 g/5 oz rice vermicelli
vegetable oil for deep frying
450 g/1 lb boneless belly of
  pork, skinned and cut into
  bite-sized pieces
1 tbsp Chinese rice wine or dry
  sherry
1 tbsp light soy sauce
3 tbsp cornflour
1 egg white
150 g/6 oz carrots, cut at
  random into bite-sized pieces
2 tbsp vegetable oil
1 tbsp sesame oil
1 medium-sized onion, cut into
  bite-sized pieces
1 green pepper, cut into bite-
  sized squares
For the sauce:
450 ml/14 fl oz chicken stock
  (see page 25)
2⅔ tbsp sugar
120 ml/4 fl oz tomato ketchup
1⅓ tbsp light soy sauce
4 tbsp Chinese rice wine or dry
  sherry
4 tbsp vinegar
salt and black pepper
2 tbsp cornflour
3 tbsp water

● Fill a wok or saucepan a quarter full of oil and heat to 180°C/350°F. Separate the vermicelli into small portions. Deep fry the vermicelli in several batches in the wok. They puff up in a few seconds, so be ready to take them out promptly. Drain on absorbent paper. Put the crispy vermicelli on to four plates and lightly crush.

● Marinate the pork in the rice wine and soy sauce for 20–30 minutes. Mix 2 tablespoons of the cornflour, the egg white and 1 teaspoon of water together in a bowl and coat the pork with the cornflour mixture. Deep fry the meat for about 4–5 minutes or until golden brown. Drain on absorbent kitchen paper, then crush lightly and arrange on 4 plates.

● Cook the carrots in a pan of boiling water for about 15 minutes and set aside. Heat 1 tbsp of the vegetable oil and 1 tbsp of the sesame oil in the wok or frying pan until very hot. Stir fry the onion and green pepper for 1–2 minutes, add the carrots and stir for a further minute.

● Add the chicken stock, sugar, tomato ketchup, soy sauce and rice wine and bring to the boil. Add the vinegar and season.

● Combine the cornflour with the water and stir well into the sauce. Add the pork. Scoop the sweet and sour pork on to the noodles and serve.

pork and pineapple in honey sauce on crispy vermicelli

Another dish with a sweet and sour theme. The honey and pineapple complement the pork very well.

125 g/5 oz rice vermicelli
vegetable oil for deep frying
450 g/1 lb boneless belly of
  pork, skinned and cut into
  bite-sized pieces
salt and black pepper
1 tbsp Chinese rice wine or dry
  sherry
2½ tbsp cornflour
2 tbsp water
For the sauce:
2 tbsp vegetable oil
2.5 cm/1 in fresh ginger, peeled
  and minced
1 clove garlic, minced
2 medium-sized onions, cubed
200 g/7 oz carrots, sliced
4 rings pineapple (tinned),
  chopped
salt and black pepper
400 ml/14 fl oz chicken stock
  (see page 25)
2 tbsp honey
2 tsp brown sugar
1 tsp light soy sauce
4 tbsp pineapple juice (from the
  tin)
2 tbsp cornflour mixed with 3
  tbsp water

● Fill a wok or saucepan a quarter full of vegetable oil and heat to 180°C/350°F. Deep fry the rice vermicelli in small batches. They will puff up in a few seconds. Drain on absorbent paper.

● Sprinkle the pork with salt and black pepper, then marinate in the rice wine for 15 minutes. Combine the cornflour and water and coat the pork with the paste. Deep fry the pork until lightly browned in the oil used for the vermicelli. Drain on absorbent paper.

● Heat the oil in the cleaned wok or frying pan. Stir fry the ginger and garlic for 30 seconds. Add the onions and carrots and stir fry for about 2 minutes. Add the pineapple, lightly sprinkle with salt and pepper and stir.

● Add chicken stock, honey, sugar, soy sauce and pineapple juice. When the sauce is boiling, add the combined cornflour and water to thicken the sauce. Add the pork and mix.

● Put the crispy vermicelli on to four plates, then lightly crush. Pour the sauce over and serve immediately.

Left

Sweet and Sour Pork on Crispy Vermicelli

Index